AF478118

Beneath the Cherry Sapling

Edited & translated by Norbert Krapf

Fordham University Press, New York   1988

ℬeneath the Cherry Sapling

LEGENDS FROM FRANCONIA

LC 88-80933

ISBN 0-8232-1212-2

Designed by Richard Hendel

Printed in the

United States of America

für

Elisabeth und Heinz Bier

aus Lohr am Main

Frankonia! Du reiches Sagenland,

Dir übergibt des Forschers reine Hand

Die Sagen, die er, dich durchwandernd froh,

In deinen Bergen, deinen Wäldern fand.

—Ludwig Bechstein

Acknowledgments

The legends collected here are translated from the following sources: Carlheinz Gräter, *Sagen und Schwänke aus Franken,* Sagen und Schwänke aus Süddeutschland 7 (Konstanz: Rosgarten Verlag, 1971); Christa Hinze and Ulf Diederichs, *Fränkische Sagen* (Düsseldorf/Cologne: Eugen Diederichs Verlag, 1980); Valentin Pfeiffer, *Spessart-Sagen* (Aschaffenburg: Paul Pattloch Verlag, 1972/1948); Franz Schickelberger, *Aus alten Zeiten: Main–Spessart-Sagen* (Würzburg: Echter Verlag, 1977); Karl Treutwein, *Sagen aus Mainfranken* (Würzburg: Stürtz Verlag, 1969). Source identifications for individual legends are given at the end of this book. Fourteen of the legends appeared, in German and English, in the editor's *Finding the Grain: Pioneer Journals, Franconian Folktales, Ancestral Poems* (Jasper, Ind.: Dubois County Historical Society, 1977), but the translations have been revised for this book. The poems "In Lohr am Main" and "Hesslar" were included in *Finding the Grain* and the editor's poetry collection *A Dream of Plum Blossoms* (West Layfayette, Ind.: Sparrow Press, 1985). Grateful acknowledgment is made to all these publishers for permission to reprint material and to the trustees of Long Island University for granting the 1984–1985 sabbatical that helped the editor move this project toward completion.

Contents

In Lohr am Main

Geraniums, geraniums
bursting into flames
in the corners of my eyes.
In geometric gardens
behind my back in the park,
in windowboxes above
my head on the street.

Painted wooden virgins
and saints huddle
in the niches on
half-timbered buildings.

A church tower,
bulwarked at the base,
climbs stone by stone
above red tile roofs.

The town wall crumbles
into ivied archways,
cobbled stones push
like the past against
the soles of my shoes.

A stocky woman sits
on the steps of her
cottage stringing
green beans in her
lap in the sun.

People greet me
in guttural words
I suddenly remember
hearing as a child.

Familiar faces awakening
from childhood dreams
invite me into old homes,
point out the shop where
the ancestral house stood.

Bells peal, tolling me
back. Geraniums, geraniums
bursting into flames.

Hesslar

Pigs grunt and squeal in a stall
in the yard as I stand at the foot

of a ladder below the loft where
the hired hands and linen weavers

who bequeathed me my name slept
beside animals whose breath warmed

their winter nights in this hill-top
village where every street and lane

dead-ends into fields they worked
like Brueghel peasants in sweat-stained

shirts and tithed their crops
to Würzburg prince-bishops before

wandering from village to village,
throwing themselves upon an alien ocean

and entering a foreign wilderness
after destroying every trace of this

obscure place except for the name
scrawled on a little girl's communion

certificate which led me back to
this village where streets dead-end

into fields and this ancient cottage
outside of which pigs grunt and squeal.

Beneath the Cherry Sapling

Introduction

When I moved away from my native Indiana in 1970, I began the research in family history that led, eventually, to the Franconian legends collected in this book. I grew up in the German town of Jasper, in the hills of Dubois County, where German had not been taught in the schools since 1917. That situation did not change until 1973, twelve years after I graduated from high school. Whatever German I picked up while living in Jasper came from hearing my parents and their relatives and friends speak a nineteenth-century variety laced with Hoosier English. At St. Joseph's College, far to the north, I crammed in a semester of German on top of an overload and learned to spell and pronounce properly some of those words I'd never seen committed to a page. After some ten years of digging, I discovered that both sides of my family—my mother was a Schmitt—had come to the United States in the 1840s from Franconia, in northern Bavaria. No one knew, until then, that my mother's and father's families once lived about twenty miles apart in Lower Franconia.

To borrow a phrase from a favorite contemporary poet, the Kansas-born William Stafford, for as long as I can remember I have been fond of "Sniffing the Region." I have always loved literature deeply rooted in a particular place— poems, stories, novels that seem to have welled up out of generations of living in a *Heimat*. My favorite route to the outer reaches of the cosmos runs right through the province, and back again. In *The Birth of the Poet*, William Everson expresses eloquently the spiritual dimension of regionalism, which he sees as

a centering device, a way of getting to a higher state
of being, participation in a greater frame of reference.
Conversely, regionalism forms a conduit back so that
the substance of the greater frame may return to the
individual. That is its real secret—not merely what
you put into the landscape, but what the landscape
puts into you [160–61].

When I moved away from the region where my family
had lived since uprooting themselves from the place or
places in Germany whose identity was still a mystery to us, I
felt a deepening need to know something concrete about my
origins. I wanted to make a connection with my ancestors
by standing where they had once lived, seeing what they
saw, hearing what they heard. Not long after I moved to the
East Coast in 1970, I began to write poetry. Ever since
then, my passion for origins has been inseparable from my
compulsion to write poems. I find it impossible to live, fully,
in the present without understanding where I have lived in
the past.

Before the "roots" phenomena occasioned in part by Alex
Haley's book of the same title, serialized on television
here and abroad, and the bicentennial hoopla surrounding
the year 1976, I discovered that my mother's family, the
Schmitts, had lived in the river town of Lohr am Main, not
far from the seat of the bishopric of Würzburg. A ship's passenger list that my wife and I found in the National Archives
in Washington, D.C., revealed that Jacob Schmitt and his
wife Anna Maria Hochgesang of "Lohr" came to the port of
Baltimore in 1840, with their six children, on the ship
America. That year, 1973, I visited Lohr for the first of

many times and met Schmitts, none directly related, who lived in the old part of town near the river, on Fischergasse. Jacob Schmitt and his elders, I learned from Lohr parish records, were *Schiffer* who worked on the Main River. We made friends with Heinz and Elisabeth Bier, then proprietors of the town bookstore, I bought collections of local "folktales," volumes by regional poets, and local histories, and I stood where I needed to stand, saw and heard some of what I needed to see and hear. I thought I had made my essential connection with the forsaken landscape.

What seemed like a culmination, however, was but a beginning. In continuing to research my family history, I came upon a father-and-son journal in the possession of the Betz family in my hometown, distant relatives on my mother's side of the family and good friends from high school. A grant from Long Island University, the first in what has become a long series of grants in support of the many stages of my "ancestral project," financed the transcription and translation of these journals by a native of Bremen, Mrs. Roswitha Waterman. The Betz family, John L. Betz tells us in his journal, lived in the village of Flieden in Hesse, not far north of Lohr. As a bicentennial contribution, I edited the journals for publication in my hometown newspaper, *The Herald*.

During this period, I was taking adult education courses in German at a Long Island high school; then, during a year as an exchange teacher, at a college of further education in Oxford, England; then at The New School in New York City; and later at the Goethe Institute in Schwäbisch Hall during the bicentennial summer. I was also at work translating some fourteen "folktales" set in and around Lohr and writing a cycle of "ancestral" poems. Other pioneer German documents surfaced in my hometown, and although I certainly had not begun with the idea of making a book out of my ancestral obsession, all of this material came together as a tripartite collection I edited, *Finding the Grain: Pioneer Journals, Franconian Folktales, Ancestral Poems* (Jasper, Ind.: Dubois County Historical Society, 1977). The local response was enthusiastic, reviews in scholarly journals were positive, and because of a resulting upswell of interest in the German heritage of the area, I was able to locate additional pioneer German journals and letters. After the book went out of print rather quickly, I decided that an expanded version was not only justified, but necessary. To be candid, I wanted badly to read such a book, knew others did too, and could see all too easily that no one else could or would take on the job. That was ten years ago, and I have been at work ever since on what I have come to realize must be *several* books, including *Beneath the Cherry Sapling*. The historical documents, including forty-two letters of Rev. Joseph Kundek, who colonized my native area with German Catholics, and a chain of twenty-two letters by members of the Hassfurther and Gerhard families, early settlers in Ferdinand, Indiana, founded by Kundek, as well as the re-edited journals and letters from the first part of *Finding the Grain,* will constitute a book titled *The Story They Wanted to Tell.* Although my academic training has been in English and American literature, I have felt an obligation to help my ancestors and their contemporaries tell the story of what it was like to come to America, and to help tell the stories or "tales" they left behind in what had been their Franconian *Heimat.*

One reviewer of *Finding the Grain* suggested that the section of Franconian folktales in that book would have been enriched by the inclusion of some "Dubois County folktales" he was sure must be extant. That made me think of the "Dubois County Dutch" stories I had heard in and around Jasper, told in a mix of German dialect of the nineteenth century and southern Indiana English, about a mythical local farmer named Ed Meyer. For inclusion in what I was then envisioning as the expanded version of *Finding the Grain,* in August of 1978 I taped Bob Steffe of Jasper telling nine Ed Meyer stories and Steffe and my father, the late Clarence Krapf, telling fifteen short humorous anecdotes about the eccentric Basil Heusler, O.S.B., a native of Switzerland who became pastor of St. Joseph's parish in 1898. It became apparent, however, that these Dubois County German tales, transcribed and "translated" by Mary Joe Meuser, a Ferdinand native who teaches German at Jasper High School, should be separated from the Franconian legends I was working on. When Eberhard Reichmann of Indiana University and the Indiana German Heritage Society announced plans to compile a collection of "Hoosier German folktales," I sent him the tapes and transcripts of the Ed Meyer and Father Basil stories.

The same month that I recorded these Dubois County tales, with the help of a first communion certificate pressed between the pages of an old German prayerbook belonging to a third cousin I had never met, Emma Bartley, I discovered that my father's family had also come from Lower Franconia. The Krapfs had been *Tagelöhner,* agricultural day-laborers, in a series of villages and hamlets in the Würzburg area: Hesslar (until 1830), once owned by the family of the prince-bishop of Würzburg and operated as an agricultural supply source for the Julius Hospital; Kreuzthal, a station of the university forest preserve where my great-grandfather Johann was born during the family's three-year stay (1830–1833); and Tugendorf, a manor that was at one time owned by the wealthy Thurn und Taxis family before it was divided and sold. Documentary evidence reveals that the Krapfs were in Tugendorf from 1834 through 1841. I have collected data establishing my family's connections with these places in the Bavarian State Archives in Würzburg, the Julius Hospital Archive in the same city, the Thurn und Taxis Central Archive in Regensburg, and a number of parish archives in Lower Franconia, most notably Hesslar. I have stood in all of these ancestral haunts, more than once, and have had a chance to look and listen. Part of what I needed to hear is contained in the legends I have gathered from various sources and translated for this book.

NOT UNTIL I reached the final stages of translating these fifty-two "Franconian folktales" into American English did I become aware that they are indeed what folklorists term "legends," "local legends," or "local traditions." I had reason, however, not to be aware of the distinction between the generic "folktale" and the more particular "legend." Even though the Brothers Grimm had published a two-volume collection of 585 *Deutsche Sagen* in 1816 and 1818, unlike the universally known and acclaimed *Märchen,* or "fairy tales," they have rarely been translated into other languages and did not even become available in English until Donald Ward's monumental two-volume *German Legends of the Brothers Grimm* appeared in 1981. Ward discusses the lives of the Brothers Grimm and their contributions to folklore, grammar, and linguistics, explains the significance of the legend form especially as manifest in Germany, provides invaluable commentaries on each of the almost 600 legends he translates, and includes a bibliography on legendry. He points out that, whereas between 1850 and 1950 some 500 collections of *Sagen* were published in German-speaking countries, "In the English-speaking world, by contrast, where the legends have never been translated and where lamentably few folklorists read German, the field is correspondingly barren" (2 : 380).

Although he chastizes the Brothers Grimm in *Fairy Tales and the Art of Subversion* for inculcating middle-class values in the process of expanding and changing the fairy tales they transcribed, Jack Zipes readily acknowledges that ever since 1812 "the Brothers Grimm have been continually looking over our shoulders and making their presence felt" (45). In the romantic prose of the "Foreword" to the first volume of their legend collection, the Grimms outline differences between the fairy tale and the legend:

> The fairy tale is more poetic, the legend is more historical; the former exists in its innate blossoming and consummation. The legend, by contrast, is characterized by a lesser variety of colors, yet it represents something special in that it adheres always to that which we are conscious of and know well, such as a locale or a name that has been secured through history. Because of this local confinement, it follows that legend cannot, like the fairy tale, find its home anywhere [Ward 1 : 1].

If the legend as a genre cannot find its home in just one place, the characters in legends are, according to Max Lüthi in his 1947 *The European Folktale* (translated into English earlier this decade) irrevocably bound to their place of origin, to their "home":

> The protagonists of legends live and work in their native village. They do not leave it, but rather live and experience, act and dream at home. Here they have their most important relationships, with their village companions and with a wholly other world. The scenes where the events of the legend take place are familiar to them from childhood, whether these are the fields, meadows, and streams of their village, or its houses and its church, or the neighboring woods. . . . When the people of legendry do leave home, they are gripped by a feeling of homesickness that drives them irresistibly homeward until they begin to feel themselves grow well again [16].

Because the legend is grounded in the local, because it is so concrete and specific, it is a variety of tale that might seem to be limited in range and scope. As Dan Ben-Amos has noted in his Foreword to Ward's first volume, however, "The specificity of legends is deceptive. While these tales are often told about particular places or particular persons, tales with almost identical themes and structures are told about other locations and other individuals" (x). Wherever people have lived, it would seem, legends have arisen, as if from a universal spring.

In a "Folkloristic Commentary" included in a popular edition of *The Complete Grimms' Fairy Tales,* Joseph Campbell sees a connection between the specific or local setting and the memory-hauntedness that characterize the legend:

8

"*Sage* designates any little local story, associated with this or that specific hill or grove, pond or river. By a people inhabiting a spirit-haunted and memory-haunted landscape, the *Sage* is conceived to be a recitation of fact" (841). The telling of something extraordinary, even supernatural, as if it actually happened, is one of the distinguishing features of the legend. According to Ward, specific names, places, and dates are essential for the creation of this effect of credibility or verisimilitude so important to the legend (2:374). The extraordinary and the factual, Stith Thompson implies in his classic study *The Folktale,* lie down together in the legend:

> This form of tale purports to be an account of an extraordinary happening believed to have actually occurred. It may recount a legend of something which happened in ancient times at a particular place—a legend which has attached itself to that locality but which will probably also be told with equal conviction of many other places. . . . It may tell of an encounter with marvelous creatures which the folk still believe in—fairies, ghosts, water-spirits, the devil, and the like. And it may give what has been handed down as memory—often fantastic or even absurd—of some historical character [8].

But what, one might ask, is the typical subject matter of a legend? A legend, it stands to reason, must be interesting enough to engage the listener's attention; it must therefore be about something important and vital. In his "Epilogue," Ward establishes a relationship between the subject matter of legends and their frequently moralistic, didactic, cautionary tone:

Another characteristic of the legend is that it is invariably the direct expression or reflection of the most dominating concerns and cherished values of the members of the communities in which it is told. Legends will thus focus upon such economic matters as the production of dairy cattle, and the forces that threaten the yield of milk and butterfat; or maleficent magic that destroys crops; on sinners who move border stones, thus occasioning the gain of valuable property by one farmer at the cost of another. Legends also focus upon the outrageous violation of behavioral norms and the retribution of human or divine forces against the perpetrators; as such, one can find elements of social protest in legends. For the most part, however, the tradition tends to be conservative in upholding the moral order and the status quo in general [2:374].

LIKE the legends collected by the Brothers Grimm, the fifty-two I have translated feature a strong moralistic sense and warn listeners against some kind of excess or violation of secular or sacred law. Over a dozen deal directly with "crime and punishment," with human or divine retribution for some kind of wrong-doing. Stealing and swindling, especially when the poor are victimized, are severely punished; the culprit is transformed, with almost no hope of release or salvation, into a swine, a black hellhound, a trapped spiderman, a drudging ghost. Excessive drinking—surely quite a temptation in a region producing superb but regrettably seldom-exported wines—provokes sudden illness or death, of the reveler or his next of kin (a particularly reprehensible excess when the sinner is in a position of authority), or can turn a person into a murderer or murder victim. An abundant supply of wine can even provoke a nocturnal attack by "the wild army," that horde of condemned souls. A "Thou Shalt Not" message is loud and clear.

Another violation singled out for punishment is blasphemy or failure to fulfill a religious obligation. Missing Mass because of "hunting fever," a malady that seems almost epidemic in the forests of *Unterfranken,* defiling the sanctity of a cemetery, cursing one's misfortune—these merit condemnation to the "ghostly hunt" of lost souls wandering the wilds, the onslaught of a mysterious illness, or the precipitous death of one's child. One tale ends with a nice ironic twist: a knight is so dehumanized by a fit of hunting fever that he loses all compassion for his fellow man, whereupon the compassionate beggar he has spurned rescues him from the depths of the dark forest—from the depths of himself.

There are tales of treasure buried on the site of ruins. Typically, the treasure-hunters encounter obstacles in the form of a ghost or devil guardian, they get burned (sometimes literally) because of their greed, or clubbed for their dishonesty and unworthiness. As the result of a temporary blindness, they walk away with only a small amount of the treasure after having forgotten the key to the vault, or they may find that the treasure simply vanishes.

Included here are a number of saints' legends (Burkhard, Pippin, Gertrude, Cecilia). There are tales in which a special day of the liturgical calendar (Maunday Thursday, Corpus Christi, St. George's Day, Christmas) provides the occasion for a supernatural event, or a child born on a special day (Sunday) has unique powers, or the ringing of the angelus bell or a local church bell has special significance or effects. There are miracle legends in which the Christ child appears, the Virgin protects those who honor her and her sacred image, coals turn to coins on a saint's day, and a ghostly priest appears to say Mass at the "witching hour," midnight. The goat-footed devil appears to a fisherman, boys who go poaching at night, Catholics who go to Lutheran services, and a schnapps-drinking miller who boasts that he is unafraid of death. The devil even whacks one lying, potato-thieving (horrible abomination!), treasure-hunting youth on the head.

Predictably for an area so steeped in Catholicism, the clergy appear frequently in these legends, sometimes as sinners in need of warning or deserving of retribution. One example, which combines treatment of courtly pageantry, a tournament, and anti-clerical bias, deserves to be singled out. The lovely prize lady in "The Long Barrier" turns out, in the end, to be a "water spirit," a mermaid who slithers away from the knight who desires her above all others, and plunges into the Main River, inspiring the "victorious" knight to abandon this world and become a monk in a strict order.

There are a few tales of magic, not always "black." An alchemist turns a horseshoe into gold in payment for a debt, a shepherd manages to flog an obnoxious raftsman from across the Main River, and a wondrous bird warns the only survivor of a plague-stricken community to rub himself with a certain herb and thus escape death. Witches appear in the guise of a black cat and a tanner's cook, ghosts assume various animal shapes, and dwarves outwit and punish an inn-keeper who dilutes his wine with water.

A few of the legends explain how or why something was created or begun and are thus "etiological." Individual tales explain the origin of a town crest, caricature statues outside a local church, and an order of noble nuns. There are historical legends inspired by skirmishes and acts of piracy during the Peasants' Revolt and the revelry and laziness of some students at the famous university in Würzburg.

As suggested above, the hunt is often the subject of or a motif in these Franconian legends. In one tale already referred to, hunting fever reduces the humanity of one nobleman and prevents him from observing his religious duties. More often than not, the hunt puts the individual under the influence of demonic forces, as in the tale about youths who go poaching at night, a violation of the property and privilege of nobility, or makes the hunter into a demonic being who hacks off a human hand to leave as a gift for innocent woodsmen. In one tale a hunter who narrowly escapes being killed by a rampaging wounded boar compensates for his rather providential salvation by placing a saint's image in the hole of a treetrunk. In yet another, exactly a year to the day after a large roebuck is shot on Corpus Christi, a roebuck appears on a village street, miraculously survives, unscathed, two shots fired at close range, and disappears before the eyes of the whole community; the equation of the buck with the body and supernatural powers of Christ is unmistakable. Nowhere is the association of the hunt with the forces of darkness more clear-cut than in a tale of a "ghostly huntsman," a "Wild Hunt." A party of lords and knights had forsaken their spiritual duty on a holy day of obligation to go on the hunt and are now condemned to repeat for all eternity their "wicked hunting procession" in full regalia above the towers of the abbey.

One memorable legend with an element of social commentary combines the excesses of hunting and drunkenness with the motif of the Robber Baron. The knight in question lived at the end of the Middle Ages when chivalry was in decline. He abandons himself more and more to drinking and hunting, rapes the daughter of a forester, moves her to commit suicide, and becomes a highwayman. Eventually the knight-robber, confronted and cornered by his count, punishes himself for his wicked ways. He leaps in full armor into the "abyss" below the castle. His ghost is said to haunt the ruins during the full moon, cursing and blaspheming.

Because I came to these Franconian legends through an extended process of discovering ancestral ties with particular places, I considered grouping them by setting: Lohr am Main, Würzburg, Hesslar, etc., or the more general The Spessart, The Main Valley from Würzburg to Schweinfurt, The Steigerwald, Bamberg and the Hassberge. There would have been some justification in doing so. German collections of legends, such as the Franconian ones from which many of these are taken, are often divided into sections according to place. But the editors of these collections are more consistent than I have wanted or could pretend to be. Whereas the editors of these German collections no doubt methodically gathered all the legends they could find about a particular place or region, I selected what struck me as the best, most interesting legends set in and around the villages,

towns, and one city, the nearby cultural, religious, and po-
litical center, Würzburg, connected with the life of my ancestors. In retrospect it seems naïve to have considered
that an obsession with ancestral haunts might yield a book
evenly balanced between a number of such places.

Although I feared that their sometimes overlapping "types
of tales" and classification of "motifs" would not contain my
ancestral passion, in the end folklorists provided me with a
principle of arrangement. Ronald L. Baker, compiler and
editor of the invaluable *Hoosier Folk Legends* (1982) and
Jokelore: Humorous Folktales from Indiana (1986), concedes
in the introduction to the former: "Because of their great
variety, legends are no easier to classify than to define" (2).
Baker finds that the four general categories of legends tenta-
tively proposed at an international folklore conference in
Budapest in 1963 "are not especially useful in organizing
collections of American legends" (3). He therefore employs
four general categories that apply to Indiana legends: supernatural and religious legends; personal legends; place legends; and modern legends. Following Baker's practice of
adapting categories to suit the material in hand, I have orga-
nized my Franconian legends into five sections determined
by theme: 1) Crime and Punishment; 2) Ghosts, Witches,
Devils, Sprites; 3) Saints, Holy Days, Special Liturgical
Days; 4) Tales Historical and Etiological; 5) Treasure Hunts.
To be sure, there may be a devil lurking in a tale of Crime
and Punishment (No. 12), an historical/etiological tale
might include a saint (No. 40) or refer to a special liturgical
day (No. 44), and treasure hunts might contain a saint or
saint's day (No. 49), or include both a ghost and a special

religious day (No. 51); but by and large these five categories stand with reasonable integrity. I believe that they will also make good reading for the layman and scholar alike.

In the Preface to *Finding the Grain* I generalized about what I hoped to accomplish in my translation of the fourteen Franconian legends, since revised, that became the genesis of this book: "Anyone who translates folktales or reads them in translation comes to realize that a too literal translation stifles the vitality, mood, and feeling of the original. I have tried to be as free as I could without sacrificing the meaning of the German versions facing the translations" (9). Ten years later and the twenty translations of *Shadows on the Sundial: Selected Early Poems of Rainer Maria Rilke* behind me, I find the word "free" offensive. I would now prefer to say "natural." I want my translations to sound as though they were spoken by an American, perhaps of German descent, but I do not want to take liberties. The German versions facing my translations stand as witness to where these legends came from and as reminder of the ancestral language I have had to learn in order to midwife them into my mother tongue.

I want to thank Bernd Engler, my colleague for a year in the English Department of the University of Freiburg, Eberhard Reichmann of the Department of Germanic Studies, Indiana University, Bloomington, and Giles Hoyt, Department of German Language and Literature, Indiana University–Purdue University, Indianapolis, for blowing whistles on errors in the original fourteen translations and others that were about to creep into some of the thirty-eight new ones I completed for this book. I would also like to thank Joe

Salmons of the Foreign Language Department, Purdue University, for his encouragement, Geoffrey Berresford and the C. W. Post Research Committee, Long Island University, for their patient and continuing support of a project that could have been seen as poaching in the forest of others, John Digby of Oyster Bay via London for opening his doors and covers into the world of the German woodcut, and the staffs of the Prints and Photographs and the Rare Book and Manuscripts Divisions of the New York Public Library for guiding my explorations in that fascinating world.

With all the help I have received in completing this project, I cannot claim to have worked any special magic, even though, to echo a detail from one of my favorite legends (No. 51), I was born on a Sunday. I may not have discovered the treasure of these legends buried under a single cherry sapling and I may not have released any ghosts; but I do feel that in putting together this book I have contributed to the rebuilding of a castle of sorts. I feel immeasurably richer for the effort and hope to witness other such restorations.

Finally, it would be disingenuous of me not to confess what a great pleasure it has been to discover, read, translate, and share these Franconian legends of my ancestral past. May the pleasure I have had be contagious and infect as many people as possible!

Norbert Krapf

Roslyn, Long Island

WORKS CITED

Baker, Ronald L. *Hoosier Folk Legends*. Bloomington: Indiana University Press, 1982.

——. *Jokelore: Humorous Folktales from Indiana*. Bloomington: Indiana University Press, 1986.

Campbell, Joseph. "Folkloristic Commentary." *The Complete Grimms' Fairy Tales*. New York: Pantheon Books, 1944, 1972. Pp. 815–64.

Everson, William. *Birth of the Poet*. Ed. Lee Bartlett. Santa Barbara: Black Sparrow Press, 1982.

Krapf, Norbert, ed. *Finding the Grain: Pioneer Journals, Franconian Folktales, Ancestral Poems*. Jasper, Ind.: Dubois County Historical Society, 1977.

Lüthi, Max. *The European Folktale: Form and Nature*. Tr. John D. Niles. Philadelphia: Institute for the Study of Human Issues, 1982.

Stafford, William. *Brother Wind*. Rexburg, Idaho: Honeybrook Press, 1986.

Ward, Donald, ed. and trans. *The German Legends of the Brothers Grimm*. 2 vols. Philadelphia: Institute for the Society of Human Issues, 1981.

Zipes, Jack. *Fairy Tales and the Art of Subversion: The Classical Genre for Children and the Process of Civilization*. New York: Wildman Press, 1983.

I Crime and Punishment

Der Hirschwirt in Lohr

Im Lohrer Gasthaus „Zum Hirschen" war vor langen Jahren ein Wirt, der oft Wasser unter den Wein mischte und diesen als echt verkaufte. Eines Tages kamen in die Gaststube drei Männer, klein von Gestalt und mit langen Bärten. Jedes der Männlein bestellte einen guten Schoppen Wein, und was tat der Wirt? Er setzte dem Weine nach Gewohnheit Wasser hinzu und brachte die gefüllten Gläser auf den Tisch.

Die drei Männer aber waren aus dem Geschlecht der Zwerge und erkannten sogleich den Betrug. Sie flüsterten miteinander, nickten ernst dazu, und hernach sprach der eine laut: „Der Weinfälscher muß hinein!" Der Wirt, der hinter der Theke stand, war aufmerksam geworden und fragte: „Wer soll hinein?"—„Der betrügerische Wirt", sagte der zweite Zwerg kurz und noch lauter als der erste. „Wohin soll er denn?" fuhr der Hirschwirt spöttisch fort.—„In den Krug", schrie jetzt der dritte mit Donnerstimme, und in derselben Sekunde wurde der Wirt in einen großen Weinkrug gebannt. Den schleppten die Zwerge in den Wald hinaus und vergruben ihn unter einem hohen Baum. Schon mancher, der hier vorbeiging, vernahm das Jammern des alten Hirschwirtes. Doch keiner hat noch das richtige Wort zu seiner Erlösung gefunden.

I The Innkeeper of "The Stag" in Lohr

Many, many years ago in the Lohr inn called "The Stag," there was an innkeeper who often mixed water in his wine and sold it as pure vintage. One day three small men with long beards came into the tavern. Each of the little men ordered a big glass of wine, and what did the innkeeper do? As usual, he poured water in the wine and brought brimming glasses to the table.

But the three men were of the race of dwarfs and recognized the swindle right away. They winked at one another, nodded in earnest, and the first one said out loud: "The wine-faker must come inside." The innkeeper jumped to attention behind the bar. "Who should come inside?" he asked. "That thief of an innkeeper," said the second dwarf abruptly, even louder than the first. "Inside where should he come?" jeered the innkeeper. "Inside the crock!" cried the third in a thunderous voice, and instantly the innkeeper was banished into a huge wine crock.

The dwarfs dragged this crock into the forest and buried it beneath a tall tree. And in fact many a person passing by there has heard the wailing of the old innkeeper of "The Stag." But no one has ever found the right word for his salvation.

Die Erscheinung im Bischofspalast

Es ist schon lange her, da hatten die Bamberger einen Fürstbischof, der war nicht eben unrecht, aber auch nicht gar so fromm wie ein Bischof sein soll und mehr aufs Trinken als aufs Fasten bedacht. Sein Vater hat auch noch gelebt und war recht rüstig.

Eines Abends gab der Bischof ein Fest, bei dem der Wein reichlich floß. Es war schon Mitternacht, als der Bischof einen Diener ins Vorzimmer schickte, um Karten zu holen. Nach einer kleinen Weile kehrte der Diener ganz verdattert und kreidebleich zurück und sagte: „Ach, Bischöfliche Gnaden, draußen auf dem Stuhl sitzt ihr Herr Vater, der hat ein langes Hemde an und ganz starre Augen."

Der Bischof schimpfte den Diener tüchtig aus und ging selbst zur Tür, da sah er draußen im Vorzimmer seinen Vater, ganz wie's der Diener beschrieben hatte, aber gleich darauf war er nicht mehr da.

Am nächsten Tag ist dem Bischof angesagt worden, daß sein Vater in der Nacht, eben um die Stunde, wo er sich im Palast sehen ließ, gestorben war. Darnach ist der Bischof mehr in sich gekehrt und viel geistlicher geworden.

2 The Apparition in the Bishop's Palace

A long time ago the people of Bamberg had a prince–bishop who wasn't exactly bad, but just wasn't as pious as a bishop ought to be. To tell the truth, he gave more thought to drinking than fasting. His father, a sprightly man, was still alive.

One evening the Bishop threw a party and the wine was flowing freely. It was already midnight when the Bishop sent a servant into an ante-room to fetch a deck of cards. After a little while the servant came back flabbergasted, pale as chalk, and said: "Your Grace, your father is sitting outside on a chair! He has on a long shirt and just stares."

The Bishop scolded the servant vigorously, went to the door himself, and saw, outside in the ante-room, his father exactly as the servant had described. In a split second, however, he was gone.

The very next day the Bishop was told that his father had died just at the moment when he appeared so mysteriously. After that the Bishop became more meditative and devoted himself more to spiritual concerns.

Der nächtliche Ruf

Der Bürgermeister von Bamberg war ein kernfester Mann und auch noch nicht alt. Einmal hatte er abends noch eine Besprechung in Gemeindesachen gehabt, danach mußte natürlich noch ein Schoppen getrunken werden, und so war es späte Nacht geworden. Der Bürgermeister wohnte hinterm Domplatz, wo jedes Kind weiß, daß es bei Nacht nicht richtig ist. Wie er nun das Dombergl hinaufgeht, hört er sich von rückwärts dreimal laut beim Namen gerufen. Er schaute sich um und suchte, aber niemand war zu sehen und alles wieder still. Da ist der Bürgermeister sehr ernst nach Hause gegangen und hat seinen Leuten gesagt: „Paßt auf, das bedeutet mir was.“ Und richtig ist er drei Tage drauf am Schlag gestorben.

3 The Cry in the Night

The mayor of Bamberg was a hale and hearty man who wasn't very old. One evening he went to a meeting on community business, and, as he of course had to have a big glass of wine afterward, it grew very late. The mayor lived behind the cathedral square where, as every child knows, it's spooky at night. As he was going up the cathedral hill, he heard his name called out loudly, three times, from behind. He turned around and looked all over, saw no one, and everything was again quiet. The mayor went home solemnly and told his people, "Mark my words, that's an omen for me!" Sure enough, three days later he died of a stroke.

Die fünf Musikanten von Falkenstein

Nahe bei Falkenstein stehen neben der Donnersdorfer Landstraße fünf Kreuzsteine, die man die „fünf Musikanten" nennt. Auf der Falkensteiner Kirchweih sollen einst sieben Musikanten zum Tanz aufgespielt haben. Sie sprachen wacker dem Most zu, wurden warm und kamen auf dem Heimweg in argen Streit. Fünf von ihnen wurden dabei erschlagen und von den Leuten kurzerhand an Ort und Stelle eingescharrt. Den sechsten Musikanten fand man tot neben der Straße von Donnersdorf nach Haßfurt. Auch dort steht ein Kreuzstein. Der siebte scheint am Leben geblieben zu sein.—Um 1840 wurde in der Nähe der fünf Steine ein Hopfengarten angelegt. Dabei fand man zwei Totenköpfe und sonstiges menschliches Gebein, gab es aber sogleich wieder der Erde zurück.

4 The Five Musicians from Falkenstein

Along the main road to Donnersdorf, just outside Falkenstein, stand five stone crosses called "The Five Musicians." Seven musicians were once supposed to have played at a dance for the Falkenstein church fair. They hit the new wine pretty hard, became hot-headed, and got into a terrible fight on the way home. Five of them were killed instantly and buried, without ceremony, right on the spot. The sixth musician was found dead farther along the road from Donnersdorf to Hassfurt where there's also a stone cross. The seventh seems to have survived. About 1840 a field of hops was planted near the five stones. On the site two skulls were found, and other human bones, but they were put right back into the earth.

Das weiße Männlein

In der Gegend von Ezelheim war einmal ein Müller, der hatte zwei Knechte und eine Magd. Die Knechte waren's gewohnt, alle Abend ihr Bier zu trinken, und die Magd mußte es ihnen holen. Der kürzeste Weg zum Wirtshaus führte über den Kirchhof, und den ging sie unbekümmert. Das kam selbst den Knechten frevelhaft vor. Die Magd aber lachte und meinte, sie komme schon durch.

Wie sie nun das nächstemal über den Kirchhof Bier holen ging, stand auf einmal ein weißes Männlein am Bahrhaus. Andere wären wohl zu Tod erschrocken, die Müllersmagd aber rief dem Männlein zu: „Paß auf, du! Wenn ich wieder zurückkomme, nehme ich dir dein Käpplein!" Und als sie auf dem Rückweg dem Männlein wieder begegnete, riß ihm die Magd das weiße Käpplein vom Kopf und nahm es mit nach Hause.

Von da an erschien jede Nacht das weiße Männlein vor dem Fenster zur Magdkammer und rief: „Gib mir mein Käpplein, gib mir mein Käpplein!" Die Magd aber dachte, was geht mich das an. Eines Nachts kam das weiße Männlein schließlich zornig in die Kammer und holte sich das Käpplein. Die Müllersmagd aber fand man am andern Morgen schreckensbleich in ihrem Bett, und bald darauf ist sie gestorben.

5 The Little White Man

Once upon a time in the vicinity of Ezelheim there was a miller who had two bounden-servants and a maid. These servants liked to drink their beer every evening and the maid had to go get it. The quickest way to the inn was through the cemetery, which she took without a second thought. Even to the servants, this seemed sacrilegious. The maid, however, just laughed and said she would make it without any problems.

As she was crossing the cemetery the next time to fetch their beer, a little white man stood at the mortuary. While others would have been scared to death, the miller's maid instead shouted to the little man: "Hey, watch out, you! On my way back I'm going to steal your little cap!" When she met him on the way back, the maid snatched the white cap off his head and took it along with her.

Every night thereafter the little man appeared at the window of the maid's quarters and cried, "Give me back my cap! Give me my cap." But the maid merely thought, "What's it to me?" One night the little white fellow finally came angrily into her chamber and fetched his cap. The next morning they found the miller's maid in her bed, white as a sheet, and soon thereafter she died.

Der Ritter von Partenstein

Zur Zeit des Faustrechtes wohnte auf der Burg Partenstein der Ritter Rolf. Er vertrieb sich den Tag mit der Jagd im weiten Forst, und abends schwang er im Kreise von Zechkumpanen den Humpen Wein.

Beim Streifen durch die Wälder begegnete ihm einst die Tochter des Waldhüters, und weil sie ihm gefiel, schmeichelte er ihr mit schönen Worten, und schließich betörte er sie und tat ihr Schande an. Der Jammer des Mädchens ließ ihn kalt, und er höhnte und verlachte es noch, so daß es aus Verzweiflung den Tod suchte. Von jetzt an trieb Ritter Rolf das Jagen noch wilder und toller als bisher, und auch dem Trunke ergab er sich immer mehr. Zuletzt sank er zum Schnapphahn und Wegelagerer herab. Er versteckte sich mit seinen Leuten in den Lohrer Waldungen, überfiel die vorbeiziehenden Kaufleute und beraubte sie. Mancher Reisende mußte im finsteren Burgturm schmachten, ehe er sich durch hohes Lösegeld befreien konnte.

Der Graf von Rieneck warnte als Lehensherr den entarteten Rittersmann; allein der kümmerte sich nicht darum und plünderte weiter. Da sagte ihm der Graf die Fehde an. Er umstellte mit seinen Reisigen die Burg, drang nach längerer Belagerung in dieselbe ein und ließ die Besatzung niederhauen. Rolf schlug in wilder Tapferkeit um sich, mußte aber vor der Übermacht auf den Söller zurückweichen und sprang, als es kein Entrinnen mehr gab, mit voller Rüstung in den Abgrund und zerschmetterte. Die Burg wurde vollständig zerstört.

Etliche Leute behaupteten später, sie hätten den so elend umgekommenen Raubritter in Vollmondnächten auf den Trümmern der Burg sitzen sehen. Andere erzählten, sie hät-

6 The Knight from Partenstein

Back in the time when clubs were more powerful than the law, the knight Rolf lived in the castle at Partenstein. He whiled away the day hunting in the vast forest, and evenings he hoisted the wine tankard with his drinking mates.

On a raid through the woods he once met the daughter of the forest ranger; and, because he fancied her, he wooed her with sweet words, eventually beguiled her, and disgraced her. The misery of the maid left him cold, and he sneered and even laughed at her. In her despair she chose to die. From that time on, the knight Rolf gave himself up more savagely and wantonly than ever before to hunting and gave in more and more to drunkenness. Eventually he became a highwayman. He hid himself with his band in the Lohr woodlands, attacked the merchants passing by, and robbed them. Many travelers had to languish in dark dungeons before they were finally ransomed.

In his official capacity as feudal lord, the Count of Rieneck warned the degenerate knight, who couldn't have cared less and pillaged even more. Then the Count declared a feud. He surrounded the castle with his knights and troops, after a prolonged siege entered by force, and had the defenders killed on the spot. Rolf girded himself with an even more ferocious courage, but, because of the attackers' superior strength, had to retreat to the central tower; as there was no escape, he finally leaped in full armor into the abyss below and was smashed to bits. The castle was completely destroyed.

Some people later claimed they had seen the robber–knight who had met such a miserable end sitting upon the

ten gehört, wie er fluchte und lästerte, und Ängstliche meiden in weitem Bogen den Platz, an welchem die Burg gestanden war.

castle ruins in the full moon. Others said they had heard him cursing and blaspheming. Fearful folk keep a safe distance from the site upon which the castle had stood.

Der verfluchte Weinstock

Vor langer Zeit hackte ein Bauer aus Gaibach an einem Frühlingsabend in seinem Weinberg. Als vom Dorf die Abendglocke herüberklang, hing er seine Mütze an einen Rebstock und sprach sein Gebet. Wenig später ging er heim, vergaß aber seine Mütze mitzunehmen.

In der Nacht gab es einen scharfen Frost. Als der Bauer am Morgen in seinen Weinberg ging, sah er, daß alle Stöcke erfroren waren. Nur der von seiner Mütze behütete Stock war frisch und grün geblieben. Da fluchte der Bauer: „Hats der Teufel so weit geholt, so soll er vollends alles holen!“, und zertrat den Stock.

Die Witterung war in diesem Jahr günstig. Überall trieben die erfrorenen Reben wieder aus, und im Oktober hing ein reicher Herbst an den Stöcken. Hochgestimmt lud der Bauer seine Fuhre voll, setzte sein einziges Kind obenauf und trieb die Pferde zum Heimweg an. Wie aber das Fuhrwerk an dem verfluchten Weinstock vorüberkam, scheuten die Pferde auf einmal und rasten den Berg hinunter. Zuletzt stürzte der Wagen mit den randvoll gefüllten Butten und Kufen um und erdrückte das Kind. Ein Bildstock an der Gartenmauer von Öttershausen bezeichnet heute noch die Unglücksstelle.

7 The Cursed Grapevine

A long time ago a farmer from Gaibach was hoeing in his vineyard on a spring evening. When the Angelus bell rang out from the village, he hung his cap on a grapevine and said his prayer. A little later he went home, but forgot to take his cap along.

That night there was a heavy frost. When the farmer went out to his vineyard in the morning, he saw that all the vines were frozen. Only the vine protected by his cap had stayed fresh and green. The farmer cursed, "Since the devil got almost everything, he might as well have the rest," and he crushed the vine to bits.

That year the weather was favorable. Everywhere the frozen grapevines sprouted again, and in October a rich harvest hung on the vines. In the highest of spirits the farmer loaded his wagon full, sat his only child on the top, and urged the horses back home. But as the wagon came past the cursed grapevine, the horses suddenly panicked and tore off down the hill. The wagon finally turned over with the overflowing vats and barrels and crushed the child. A shrine at the garden wall of Öttershausen still marks the site of the tragedy.

Der ungetreue Kornmesser

Das was für die Bauern ein schlechtes Jahr gewesen. Ein nasser Sommer hatte das Getreide auf den Feldern faulen lassen. Die Menschen in der Stadt begannen zu hungern. Es konnte nicht mehr lange dauern, und das große Sterben würde beginnen.

Da ließ der Rat der Stadt Würzburg den großen Kornspeicher öffnen und an die armen Leute Getreide ausgeben. Der Kornmesser aber, der die Aufsicht führte, war ein ungetreuer Verwalter. Bei Nacht verkaufte er heimlich mehrere Fuhren des kostbaren Gutes an die Heidingsfelder Händler. So bereicherte er sich, schädigte die Stadt und brachte die Armen um ihr bitternotwendiges Stücklein Brot. Als er zum Sterben kam, holte ihn dafür der Teufel.

Weil er den Frevel in einer Gründonnerstagsnacht begangen hatte, muß er nun jedes Jahr in dieser Nacht zwischen 11 und 12 Uhr in der Korngasse umgehen. Mit einem schweren Sack Korn auf dem Rücken und einer Metze Weizen in der Hand keucht er vom Kornspeicher die Straße hinauf bis zum Reuererkloster und denselben Weg wieder zurück. Nur ein Sonntagskind kann ihn erlösen, wenn es ihm seine Last abnimmt. Das hat aber bis heute noch niemand gewagt, denn die Augen des Gespenstes sind groß und unheimlich und funkeln wie Fensterscheiben, in denen sich ein nächtlicher Brand spiegelt.

8 The Unfaithful Grain-Measurer

It had been a terrible year for farmers. A rainy summer had left the grains rotting in the fields. The people in the city began to starve. If things didn't change there was sure to be large-scale death.

So the council of the city of Würzburg opened the big granary and gave out grain to the poor. But the grain-measurer who supervised the operation was an unfaithful steward. By night he sold, in secret, extra wagonloads of the precious goods to Heidingsfeld merchants. Thus he filled his own pockets, cheated the city, and deprived the poor of their sorely needed scraps of bread. When he died, the devil came and got him for that.

As he committed the evil deed on a Maundy Thursday night, every year on this night between eleven and twelve o'clock he has to make a round on Grain Street. With a heavy sack of grain on his back and a bundle of wheat in his hand, he wheezes from the granary up the street to the Carmelite monastery and back again the same way. Only a child born on Sunday can save him by removing his load. Up to this time no one has ever dared to do that, however, for the eyes of this ghost are large and sinister and flash like a catastrophic night fire reflected in window panes.

Die Frau Amtmann

Die Frau eines Lohrer Amtmannes war über die Maßen geizig und hatte für die Armen kein Herz. Kamen solche vor ihre Türe und baten um eine kleine Gabe, so jagte sie die armen Leute ohne Erbarmen fort und beschimpfte sie noch obendrein als faules, hergelaufenes Gesindel, dem die Peitsche gebühre. Anstatt die Speisereste an hungernde Menschen zu verteilen, ließ sie das übriggebliebene Essen den Schweinen in den Futtertrog werfen. Jawohl, den Schweinen!

Da geschieht es, daß die Frau stirbt. Und wie die Magd am folgenden Morgen die Schweine füttert, bemerkt sie erstaunt, daß bei den sechs Schweinen plötzlich noch ein siebentes steht und aus dem Trog schlürft. Die Magd erschrickt; denn sie kann sich's denken, wer sich zu den sechs Tieren gesellen mußte.

Es sprach sich herum, und bald wußte es die ganze Stadt, was in der Amtskellerei vor sich ging.

Die bestürzten Hausbewohner taten alles für die Seelenruhe der Verstorbenen, bis diese dann endlich erlöst wurde.

9 The Bailiff's Wife

The wife of a Lohr bailiff was extremely stingy and had no heart for the poor. Whenever they came to her door begging for a little charity, she chased them away pitilessly, calling them lazy, vagrant rabble who deserved a whipping. Instead of giving the leftovers from her table to hungry people, she had the food thrown out into the trough for the pigs. Yes, indeed, the pigs!

Then it happened that the woman died. And as her maidservant was feeding the pigs the following morning, she noticed in astonishment that along with the six pigs stood a seventh, slurping at the trough. The maidservant was terrified, for she had a notion who had had to join the six animals.

The rumor spread, and soon the entire town knew what was happening in the bailiff's cellarage.

The distraught tenants of the house did all they could to help release the soul of the deceased, until she finally found eternal peace.

Der Bettler von Mespelbrunn

Mitten im Spessart, von großen Wäldern umgeben, liegt das Wasserschloß Mespelbrunn. Hier wohnte einst ein Ritter, der so sehr der Jagdleidenschaft verfallen war, daß er kein Herz mehr für seine Mitmenschen hatte. Wieder einmal hatte sich im Schloßhof eine adlige Jagdgesellschaft versammelt, und man wollte gerade ausreiten, als auf der Zugbrücke dem Burgherrn ein zerlumpter Bettler entgegentrat und flehentlich um ein Stück Brot bat. Zornig aufbrausend wies der Ritter mit harten Worten den Bittenden ab und spornte sein Pferd, so daß der arme Mann fast unter die Hufe gekommen wäre.

Den Jägern war reiche Beute beschieden. Im Eifer des Jagens hatten sie auf Essen und Trinken vergessen. Gegen Abend wurde zum Sammeln geblasen und man ritt gemeinsam gen Mespelbrunn. Fast hatten sie das Schloß erreicht, da brach ein mächtiger Hirsch durchs Gebüsch. Noch einmal packte den Mespelbrunner die Leidenschaft, und er verfolgte das Wild. Niemand schloß sich ihm an. Allein jagte er dem Hirsch nach, der immer größeren Abstand gewann; immer tiefer geriet er in den dämmerigen Wald. Da rissen plötzlich Zügel und Sattelgurt, der Ritter rettete sich mit einem Sprung zur Erde, der Hirsch verschwand im Gehölz.

Nun stand der Mespelbrunner allein im Wald. Die Nacht war inzwischen hereingebrochen. Hunger und Durst quälten den Ritter über alle Maßen. Ratlos setzte er sich auf einen Stein. Unvermittelt trat plötzlich der Bettler vor ihn hin. Schweigend nahm er seine Halsbinde ab, riß sie in Streifen und band damit den Sattel und die Zügel fest, hielt dem Ritter die Steigbügel und wies ihm die Richtung zum Schloß. Dann endlich sagte er: „Herr, du hast nun selbst

10 The Beggar from Mespelbrunn

In the middle of the great forest of the Spessart stands Mespelbrunn, the castle surrounded by water. There once lived here a knight who had such a bad case of hunting fever that he had no feeling left for his fellow men. A noble hunting party had once again assembled in the courtyard and was about to ride out when a tattered beggar approached the lord on the drawbridge and begged him fervently for a piece of bread. Breaking into a rage, the knight rebuffed him with harsh words and spurred his horse on so that the poor man was almost trampled under its hooves.

That day the hunters were blessed with a rich bag, but in the fever of the hunt they had forgotten to eat or drink. Toward evening the assembly was sounded and they rode back together toward Mespelbrunn. They had almost reached the castle when a mighty stag broke through the brush. Once again the fever seized the knight and he pursued the wild animal. No one joined him. He chased the stag, but it kept eluding him as he went deeper and deeper into the forest. Suddenly the reins and girth snapped, the knight saved himself by jumping to the earth, and the stag disappeared into the woods.

At this point the knight from Mespelbrunn was standing all alone in the forest. Night had already fallen. Hunger and thirst tormented him beyond description. At the end of his wits, he sat down on a rock. Suddenly the beggar stepped out in front of him. He took off his collar without a word, tore it into strips, and repaired the reins and the saddle. Then he held the stirrup for the knight and pointed him in the direction of the castle. Finally he said, "Sir, you have now experienced firsthand how painful hunger and thirst

gespürt, wie weh Hunger und Durst tun. Du wirst fortan wohl keinen Bettler mehr davonjagen." Beschämt ritt der Burgherr nach Hause. Er ließ hernach alljährlich eine große Brotspende an die Armen verteilen.

can be. In the future you shall never be able to chase away
another beggar." Ashamed, the lord rode home. Every year
thereafter he doled out a generous gift of bread to the poor.

Die Geisterjagd bei Neustadt

In alter Zeit versahen die Mönche aus Kloster Neustadt den Gottesdienst in der Burgkapelle zu Rothenfels. Die Klosterherren waren auf der Burg gerngesehene Gäste und blieben oft bis zum späten Abend. So war die Nacht bereits hereingebrochen, als sich einst ein Pater auf den Heimweg machte. Nach einer Stunde Wegs—schon sah er die Türme der Abtei vor sich in den Nachthimmel ragen—hörte er aus Osten Jagdhornklang, Hundegebell und munteres Geschrei. Das Lärmen kam näher und näher, da sah der Mönch einen stattlichen Zug durch die Luft daherkommen: Voraus ritten Jäger und bliesen die Hörner, dann kamen geistliche Herren und Ritter hoch zu Roß mit blitzenden Jagdwaffen in den Fäusten, es folgten vornehme Damen auf edlen Zeltern, Knechte mit Jagdfalken auf den Fäusten und großen Hundemeuten an der Leine. Der gespenstische Zug schwebte in geringer Höhe über den Main, vorbei an dem erschrockenen Klosterherrn, und verlor sich im dunklen Spessart. Da der Pater nicht sicher war, ob es nicht ein Traum gewesen sei, schwieg er über das Erlebnis.

Doch genau ein Jahr später kam er am gleichen Feiertag zur Nachtstunde von Rothenfels zurück, und wieder begegnete ihm der gespensterhafte Jagdzug. Nun berichtete er im Kloster, was er schon zweimal erlebt hatte, und erfuhr, daß viele Jahre vorher eine vornehme Gesellschaft aus Würzburg in der Abtei zu Gast weilte, um im Klosterforst zu jagen. Diese Herrschaften waren so sehr von der Jagdleidenschaft besessen, daß sie des hohen Feiertags nicht achteten und ihn im Wald verbrachten. Zur Strafe müssen ihre Seelen diesen sündhaften Jagdzug wiederholen bis zum Jüngsten Tag.

11 The Ghostly Hunt near Neustadt

In olden times the monks at Neustadt monastery said Mass in the castle chapel at Rothenfels. The monks were always welcome guests at the chapel and often stayed until late in the evening. One time, night had already set in when one of the monks was making his way home. After walking for an hour—he could already see the abbey towers poking up into the nocturnal sky—he heard from the east the sound of hunting horns, the barking of dogs, and cheerful yelling. The noise came nearer and nearer, and the monk saw a stately procession coming through the air. Hunters rode in front blowing their horns; ghostly priests and knights followed high on their steeds, with glinting hunting weapons in their hands; then came noble ladies upon fine palfreys, servants with falcons on their wrists, and great packs of hounds on the leash. The ghostly procession hovered just barely above the waters of the Main River, passed the terrified monk, and disappeared into the dark Spessart. Since the monk thought he might have been dreaming, he never spoke about what he'd seen.

On the same holiday exactly a year later, however, the monk was coming back from Rothenfels in the dark, and the ghostly hunting party met him once again. This time he reported in the monastery what he had now witnessed twice, and he was told that many years before, a company of lords and knights from Würzburg had stayed at the monastery as guests, to hunt in the abbey forest. These noble men and women were so afflicted with hunting fever that they did not observe the solemn holy day, but spent it in the woods instead. For punishment, their souls have to repeat this wicked hunting procession until Judgment Day.

Die feurigen Männer von Schönrain

Einst gingen zwei Halsbacher Burschen des Nachts in den Schönrainwald, um zu jagen. Da begegneten ihnen zwei feurige Männer, die ihre Beine überkreuz stehen hatten. Die Burschen mußten vor Schreck in der gleichen Stellung verharren bis zwei Uhr nachts. Dann verschwanden die feurigen Männer, und die Wilderer konnten wieder nach Hause gehen. Am folgenden Morgen soll ihr Haar schneeweiß gewesen sein.

12 The Infernal Men from Schönrain

Once at night two youths from Halsbach went into the Schönrain forest to hunt. There they encountered two fiery men who had been standing with their legs crossed. In shock, the youths had to stand in the very same position until two A.M. At that point the infernal men disappeared and the poachers were able to go back home. The following morning their hair was reported to have been snow white.

Ein Pferd für einen Wald

Nördlich von Buch liegt der Eichenbühl. Der Rat der Stadt Haßfurt hatte lange vergeblich mit dem Besitzer, einem Grafen, über den Erwerb einiger Waldstücke neben dem Eichenbühl verhandelt. Bei einem seiner Besuche sah der Graf an der städtischen Mainmühle einen prächtigen Schimmel stehn. In einer jähen Laune verlangte er das schöne Pferd als Kaufpreis für den Wald, und die Haßfurter beeilten sich, den vorteilhaften Handel abzuschließen. Am Tag der Beurkundung aber ritt der Graf mit dem teuer erstandenen Roß zum Wald und gab dort in seiner Schwermut über den verschleuderten Besitz dem Pferd und sich den Todesstoß.

13 A Horse for a Woods

North of Buch lies the Eichenbühl, a small hill dense with oak. For a long time the city council of Hassfurt had been negotiating in vain with the owner, a count, for a strip of woods along the Eichenbühl. On one of his visits the Count saw a magnificent white horse standing near the town mill on the Main. On a whim he demanded the beautiful horse as the price for the woods, and the Hassfurt council quickly closed the favorable deal. On the day that the deal was consummated, however, the Count rode to the woods with the steed he had purchased so dearly and there, in his depression over the squandered property, delivered the death blow to the horse and himself.

Die Spinnwebmännlein

In der oberen Haßberggegend kann man an heißen Sommertagen um die Zeit des Elfuhrläutens auf dem Feld die Spinnwebmännlein sehen. Lautlos rücken sie mit Spaten und Hacke an die Marksteine und müssen dort hacken und schaufeln, bis die Glocke vom Dorf zwölf Uhr schlägt. Dann verschwinden sie. Es sind jene, die bei Lebzeiten heimlich Grenzsteine verrückt haben und nun im Grab solange keine Ruhe finden, bis sie ihr Unrecht wieder gutgemacht haben. Nur selten sieht sie einer, wie sie in langen Mänteln, vom Grabesmoder durchsichtig wie Spinnweben, im Sonnenbrand schaffen.

14 The Little Spiderweb Men

In the upper Hassberge region on hot summer days about the time the eleven o'clock bell rings, you can see the little spiderweb men in the field. They approach the boundary stones silently with spades and pick axes and have to hack and shovel away until the village clock strikes twelve. Then they disappear. These are the very ones who, while they were alive, secretly shifted boundary stones and now can find no rest in the grave until they have atoned for their injustice. They can be seen only once in a great while working in the burning sun in their long gowns, made transparent as spiderwebs by the mold of the grave.

itches, Ghosts, Devils, Sprites

Die Lohrer Köchin

Ein Weißgerber in Lohr hatte eine Köchin, die so gut zu kochen verstand, daß es nicht mit rechten Dingen zugehn konnte. Die einfachsten Mahlzeiten gerieten ihr zu Delikatessen, so daß sie im Verdacht stand, im Bund mit dem Teufel zu stehn.

Eines Tages kam ein Jäger zu dem Weißgerber, um Haare zu kaufen. Der Mann schickte seine Köchin mit dem Besucher auf den Speicher, wo Haare lagerten. Das Fußwerk des Jägers aber kam dem Gerber, als er hinterdrein sah, sehr merkwürdig vor. Es schienen ihm Bocksfüße zu sein. Eine halbe, eine ganze Stunde verging, ohne daß die Köchin und der Jäger wiederkamen. Da nahm der Gerber all seinen Mut zusammen und ging auf den Speicher. Dort fand er seine Köchin mit verdrehtem Hals an einem Balken aufgehängt. Der Jäger aber war spurlos verschwunden.

15 The Lohr Cook

A tanner in Lohr had a cook who knew her art so well that it seemed too good to be true. Her simplest meals turned out to be such feasts that she was suspected of having sold her soul to the devil.

One day a hunter came to the tanner to buy pelts. The man sent his cook with the visitor up to the attic, where the skins were stored. But as the tanner's eye followed the hunter's feet from below, they looked strangely like goats' hooves. A half hour, an hour passed, but the cook and the hunter didn't come back. The tanner gathered all his courage together and went up to the attic. There he found his cook hanging from a rafter with a broken neck. As for the hunter, he had disappeared without a trace.

Der unheimliche Fahrgast

In alter Zeit lebte in Lohr ein arbeitsamer und gottesfürchtiger Fischer. Zu diesem kam eines Tages ein fremder Jäger, der gegen gutes Geld verlangte, über den Main gefahren zu werden. Der Fischer kam dem Wunsch nach. Als der Fremde aber das Schiff bestieg, sank es so tief, daß fast die Wellen in das Boot schlugen. Der Fischer betrachtete nun den Jäger näher und bemerkte, daß er einen Geißfuß hatte. Da ruderte er, so schnell er konnte, um den unheimlichen Fremden loszuwerden. Er wagte auch nicht, Geld für die Überfahrt von diesem zu nehmen. Da warf ihm der unheimliche Fahrgast beim Aussteigen einen Vierundzwanziger auf die vordere Sitzbank. Und an der Stelle, wo das Geldstück hingefallen war, entstand ein tiefes Loch, das die Münze in das Holz eingebrannt hatte. Der Fischer legte daraufhin das Geldstück in den Opferstock. Den fremden Jäger hat er nie mehr gesehen.

16 The Weird Passenger

In the old days a hard-working and God-fearing fisher-man lived in Lohr. One day a hunter he didn't recognize came to him and, for quite a large sum of money, demanded that he be ferried across the Main. The fisherman complied with his wish. But as the stranger boarded the ship, it sank so low that the waves almost poured into it. The fisherman looked at the hunter more closely and noticed that he had a goat's foot. So he rowed as fast as he could, to be rid of the weird stranger. In no way was he going to accept any money for giving the ride. As he got out of the boat, the weird passenger threw a four-and-twenty piece on the fore seat. On the very spot where the coin had fallen, a deep hole formed which the coin had burned into the wood. When he saw that, the fisherman decided to put the gold coin in the poor box. Never again did he see that strange hunter.

Der Schäfer und der Flößer

Von keinem Stand will die Sage so viele übernatürliche Kräfte und Dinge wissen wie von den Schäfern, von denen das Volk glaubte, daß sie in ihrer Einsamkeit genügend Zeit hätten, sich mit übersinnlichen Künsten zu beschäftigen. Da soll einmal ein Lohrer Schäfer einen Flößer, der durch sein Spielen und Pfeifen die Herde beunruhigte, auf eine absonderliche Art verschlagen haben. Als nämlich der Flößer, der auf seinem am anderen Mainufer festgebundenen Floß saß, trotz eindringlichen Bittens sein Spiel nicht einstellen wollte, nahm der Schäfer seinen Kittel, breitete ihn auf der Wiese aus und schlug mit seinem Stecken auf ihn ein. Da will nun die Sage weiter wissen, daß im gleichen Augenblick der Flößer am anderen Mainufer vor Schmerzen laut zu schreien begann und sich gegen unsichtbare Schläge wehrte, bis der Schäfer wieder aufhörte.

17 The Shepherd and the Raftsman

Legends never have so much to say about supernatural powers and matters as when they're about shepherds. People believe that, because of their solitude, shepherds have enough time to occupy themselves with the arts of magic. Once a Lohr shepherd is supposed to have given an unusual kind of thrashing to a raftsman who was disturbing his herd with his playing and piping. When the raftsman, sitting on his raft tied to the opposite bank of the Main River, wouldn't stop playing despite urgent requests, the shepherd took off his cloak, spread it out on the meadow, and beat it with his staff. According to the legend, at that very moment the raftsman on the other bank of the Main began to cry out in pain and defend himself against invisible blows, until the shepherd quit.

Die langen Schranken

Einst kamen in Schweinfurt zu einem glänzenden Turnier viele Ritter zusammen, um ihre Kräfte zu messen, ihre Tapferkeit zu beweisen und für die Ehre ihrer Damen zu kämpfen. Einer der Ritter erblickte unter den vielen Edelfrauen auf der Tribüne eine Dame, die wohl fremd war und deren Schönheit ihn bezauberte. So weihte er sich zu ihrem Kämpfer und warf jedem den Handschuh hin, der ihr nicht den Preis der Schönheit zugestehen wollte. Alle seine Gegner warf er in den Sand und ging aus dem Turnier als Sieger hervor. Nun nahte er sich seiner Erwählten, die ein meergrünes Kleid trug, um aus ihrer Hand den Siegespreis zu empfangen. Liebreich und huldvoll lächelte sie ihn an, da merkte er, daß sie grüne Zähne hatte, und bebte zurück. Sie aber stieß einen Schrei aus und verwandelte sich vor seinen Augen in eine Wasserjungfrau. Mühselig rutschte sie auf ihrem Fischleib dem nahen Main zu, stürzte sich in die Flut und ward nicht mehr gesehen. Der enttäuschte Ritter aber legte Rüstung und Waffen ab und trat als Mönch in einen strengen Orden ein.

18 The Long Barriers

Once many knights came together in Schweinfurt for a distinguished tournament, to test their strength, prove their courage, and fight for the honor of their ladies. Looking at the many noble women on the platform, one of the knights caught sight of a lady who seemed to be from far away and whose beauty enchanted him. He proclaimed himself her warrior and threw down the gauntlet to all who would not concede the prize of her beauty. He tossed all his opponents in the sand and emerged as the victor of the tournament. Then he drew near the lady of his choice, who was wearing a sea-green dress, to accept the victory prize from her hand. She smiled at him lovingly and graciously, but then he noticed that she had green teeth and he backed off trembling. She shrieked and before his very eyes changed into a mermaid. Struggling clumsily, she slid on her fish-belly down to the nearby Main River, plunged into the current, and was never seen again. The disappointed knight laid down his arms and armor and became a monk in a strict order.

Das Wilde Heer ist durstig

Ein Würzburger Gastwirt war einst nach Randersacker hinausgefahren, um seine Weinvorräte zu ergänzen. Allzulange hatte er gebraucht, sich in den Winzerkellern durch die verschiedenen Jahrgänge und Lagen durchzusüffeln. So war es spät geworden und die Nacht lag schon über dem Maintal, als er endlich seine gefüllten Fässer mit dem Fuhrwerk heimwärts führte. Schon hatte er den halben Weg zurückgelegt, da hörte er hinter sich in der Luft wüstes Geschrei, Hundegebell und Peitschengeknall. Der schreckliche Lärm rückte näher—das konnte nur die Wilde Jagd sein! Der Würzburger hielt die Pferde an und kroch angstschlotternd unter seinen Wagen. Heulend und jauchzend fielen die nächtlichen Spukgestalten über die Fässer her, schlugen die Zapfen aus und tranken, schlürften und schmatzten in toller Lust. Als sie ihren Höllendurst gestillt hatten, stoben sie johlend davon. Erst viel später wagte sich der Wirt aus seinem Versteck hervor, glaubte die Fässer leer und fuhr betrübt nach Hause. Doch wie staunte er, als er am nächsten Tag seinen Gästen Wein aus diesen Fässern vorsetzte! Sie lobten diesen Tropfen über alles und wollten gar keinen andern mehr trinken. Und die Fässer wurden nicht leer, soviel der Wirt auch abzapfte und ausschenkte. Als er aber in seiner Freude von dem nächtlichen Spuk erzählte, war der Zauber gebrochen. Hinfort hielt er seinen Krug vergeblich unter die Faßhähne; die Fässer waren plötzlich leer.

19 The Wild Army Is Thirsty

Once upon a time a Würzburg innkeeper went to Randersacker to replenish his wine supply. He took too much time to sample the different vintages from various vineyards. It was growing late and night had already fallen on the Main Valley when he finally started for home, with full casks loaded on his cart. Halfway home, he heard strange cries, barking, and the cracking of a whip in the air behind him. The terrible noise came nearer—it could only be The Wild Hunting Party! The Würzburger stopped his horses and crawled under his wagon, shaking with fear. Howling and shrieking with joy, the spirits of the night fell upon the casks, knocked out the spigots, and drank noisily, smacking their lips in wild abandon. After they had quenched their hellish thirst, they flew away, yelling. Only much later did the innkeeper venture forth from his hiding place. Thinking the casks were empty, he went home dejected.

But he was flabbergasted the next day when he served his guests wine from these casks, and they reserved their highest praise for these drops and didn't want to drink anything else. The casks never became empty, no matter how much the innkeeper drew from them. When, in his excitement, he told about the spirits of the night, however, the spell was broken. From then on he held his mug under the spigots in vain; the casks had suddenly grown empty.

Der wilde Jäger

Einst schlugen zwei Waldarbeiter im Schönrainswald aus einem dicken Stamm einen Trog. Immer wenn es Abend wurde, drehten sie den Trog um und schliefen darunter. Eines Nachts zog der wilde Jäger auch über den Schönrainwald, ließ sich bei dem gefällten Stamm mit seinem Gefolge nieder und hielt ein Mahl ab. Als man damit fertig war, sagte er: „Denen da unten wollen wir auch etwas übriglassen." Am Morgen darauf fanden die beiden Arbeiter eine Menschenhand auf dem Trog.

20 The Wild Hunter

Once two woodsmen in the Schönrain forest hacked a trough out of a thick tree trunk. Every evening they would turn the trough over and sleep underneath it. One night the Wild Hunter passed into the Schönrain forest, settled down next to the felled tree with his party, and had a feast. When they were all finished he said, "Surely we want to leave a little something for those guys underneath that tree trunk." And the next morning the two workers found a human hand upon their trough.

Goldmacher

In der Rose zu Würzburg kehrte einmal ein landfremder Mann ein und ließ sich acht Tage bewirten, ohne etwas zu bezahlen. Da sagte ihm der Wirt, er könne ihm, einem ganz Unbekannten, nicht länger borgen, worauf der Fremde erwiderte: „Bringt mir ein Stück Eisen und glühende Kohlen her, dann will ich euch bald befriedigen." Der Wirt brachte ihm die Kohlen und ein halbes Hufeisen und mußte sich sodann auf eine halbe Stunde entfernen. Bei seiner Wiederkehr erhielt er von dem Mann als Zahlung das Hufeisen, welches zu lauter Gold geworden und doppelt und dreifach so viel wert war wie die Zeche.

21 Alchemist

In the inn "The Rose" in Würzburg a stranger put himself up once for eight days without paying anything at all. At that point the innkeeper said to him that he could not extend credit to a complete stranger any longer, whereupon the stranger answered, "Bring me a piece of iron and glowing coals, and I will soon satisfy you." The innkeeper brought him the coals and half a horseshoe and then had to go away for half an hour. Upon his return he received from the man in payment the horseshoe, which had turned to gold and was worth two and three times what he owed on his bill.

Der Betzenmüller

Am Fuß des Schönrainberges stand einst die Betzenmühle. Von ihr ist heute nur noch der Keller zu sehen. Der letzte Müller zog nach Halsbach. Er fürchtete sich nicht vor dem Tod; deshalb sagte er immer: „Wenn der Tod kommt, gebe ich ihm ein Schnäpschen, dann geht er schon wieder fort." Eines Tages nun stand der Müller auf einem kleinen Wagen, stürzte unglücklich rücklings herunter und war sofort tot. So hatte der Betzenmüller keine Zeit mehr gehabt, dem Tod ein Schnäpschen zu spendieren und mußte mit ihm gehen.

22 The Betz Miller

Once at the foot of the Schönrain mountain there stood the Betz mill. Today the cellar is all that can be seen of it. The last miller moved to Halsbach. He wasn't afraid of death and so he always said, "When Death comes, I'll give him a little schnapps—then he'll go away." One day the miller was standing on a small wagon, unfortunately fell off backward, and died instantly. So the Betz miller had no time to treat Death to a little schnapps, and had to go away with him.

Der Pestvogel

Wieder einmal ging vor vielen Jahren die Pest im Maintal zwischen Rothenfels und Langenprozelten um. Die Menschen starben wie die Eintagsfliegen. Da soll in einer Gemeinde, deren Namen nicht mehr genau bekannt ist, der letzte noch lebende Einwohner zum Friedhof gewankt sein, um sich selbst ein Grab zu schaufeln. Die Sage erzählt nun, daß er einen seltsamen Vogel am Friedhof entdeckte, der dort in der Krone eines Baumes saß, einen Vogel mit weißem Leib und schwarzem Schnabel. Und der Vogel soll gezwitschert haben: „Wiesenpimpernell, schnell, schnell!" Als das der Mann hörte, suchte er schleunigst das Kraut, womit er dann die Pest am eigenen Körper geheilt und die Bewohner des Lohrer Maintals gerettet haben soll.

23 The Plague Bird

Many years ago the plague was once again stalking the Main Valley between Rothenfels and Langenprozelten. People were dropping like May flies. In one community, whose name is not recorded, the last surviving resident is supposed to have staggered to the cemetery to dig a grave for himself. As the story goes, at the edge of the cemetery he discovered, in the top of a tree, a strange bird with a white body and a black beak. And this bird is supposed to have chirped, "Pimpernell, schnell, schnell!" * As soon as he heard this, he looked all around as fast as he could for the herb which reportedly healed his body of the plague and saved the residents of the Main Valley around Lohr.

---

* Quick.

Der Spuk auf dem Kirchpfad

In der Zeit der Reformation, als die Bewohner von Heßlar in den evangelischen Gottesdienst nach Thüngen gingen, nahm man immer denselben Weg. Der Weg hieß deshalb Kirchpfad. Alte Heßlarer erzählen von diesem Pfad, daß es dort umgehe. Besonders in stürmischen Nächten, wenn drinnen im „Säli" der Sturm durch die Bäume fährt und Wolkenfetzen übers Werntal jagen, dann sitzt auf dem Kirchpfad ein kohlrabenschwarzer Hund und bewacht einen Haufen glühender Goldstücke. Man sagt, daß der Hund ein hartherziger Heßlarer Freibauer sei, der in schlimmer Zeit der Teuerung und Hungersnot sich für ein Metzlein Korn sündhafte Wucherpreise bezahlen ließ, und gar mancher mußte hungern, weil er das Geld nicht aufbringen konnte. Der Geizhals soll ein jammervolles Ende genommen haben. Noch heute bewacht er auf dem Kirchpfad seine in himmelschreiendem Unrecht erworbenen Goldstücke.

24 The Spook on the Church Path

During the Reformation, whenever the residents of Hesslar went to the Lutheran service at Thüngen, they always took the same path. The route was therefore called the Church Path. Old Hesslarites claim that this path is haunted. Especially on stormy nights, when in the section of the fields called "Säli" the storms travel through the trees and cloud-tatters speed across the Wern Valley, a hound as black as coal sits on the Church Path and guards a pile of glowing gold coins. It's said that the dog was a cold-hearted big-shot farmer who, in the hard times of high prices and famine, demanded a sinfully exorbitant price for a peck of grain, and many people therefore had to starve because they couldn't afford to pay. The miser is supposed to have come to a miserable end. Even today he guards his sacrilegiously ill-gotten gold coins on the Church Path.

Ein verhexter Weg

Von Retzbach nach Thüngen führt ein Weg durch den Wald, der wegen seiner Unheimlichkeit bei Nacht und auch bei Tag von den Leuten alleine nicht gerne begangen wird. Auf diesem Weg erschien den einsamen Wanderern des Nachts fast regelmäßig eine Gestalt in Gehrock und Zylinder. Manch einem folgte der Geist ein Stück weit, ohne daß man sich seiner erwehren konnte. Auch tat er niemand etwas zuleide, sondern zog, an seinem Bestimmungsort angekommen, höflich den Zylinder und ließ den Wanderer allein heimwärts ziehen.

Auf dem gleichen Weg zeigten sich dann und wann noch andere Spukgestalten. Der Bauer Michael Scheeb aus Binsfeld ging eines Nachts von Stetten kommend heimzu. Da kroch auf der Thüngener Höhe ein Untier mit Hörnern, Schwanz und Bockshufen hinter einem Holzwellenhaufen hervor, und mit weitaufgerissenem Maul sprang es dem erschreckten Bäuerlein entgegen. Diesem war Hören und Sehen vergangen, und in seiner übergroßen Not stammelte er ein Stoßgebet. Und siehe da, das Untier wandte sich ab und verschwand.

25 A Bewitched Path

From Retzbach to Thüngen a path leads through the woods which people don't like to take alone because it's so scary at night and even by day. On this path at night a figure in frock coat and top hat appeared, almost regularly, to the lonesome traveler. The ghost followed many a person for just a while; you just couldn't get rid of him. To tell the truth, he never really hurt anybody, but politely lifted his top hat as he reached his destination and then let the traveler go on home alone.

Now and then other ghostly figures appeared on this path. One night the farmer Michael Scheeb of Binsfeld was on his way home from Stetten. On the peak of the Thüngen summit, a monster with horns, tail, and goat's hooves crept out from behind a huge woodpile. Mouth stretched wide open, it leaped at the terrified farmer. At that point, he didn't know whether he was coming or going and so, in his terror, he stammered a short fervent prayer. Believe it or not, that monster turned away and disappeared.

Das verbrühte Mädchen

In Rügheim lebte einmal ein Mädchen, das sich in eine Maus verwandeln konnte. Jeden Abend störte es die Nachbarn mit seinem Geraschel, daß sie kaum mehr zum Schlafen kamen. Schließlich wurde es den Leuten zu dumm. Sie lauerten der Maus auf, und als sie rasch in einem Loch verschwand, gossen sie einen Topf heißes Wasser hinterher. Am andern Morgen jammerte die Mutter des Mädchens, ihre Tochter habe sich den Leib verbrüht. Da wußten die Nachbarn, wer das Mäuslein gewesen war, und von da an hatten sie ihre Ruhe.

26 The Scalded Girl

There once lived in Rügheim a girl who could turn into a mouse. Every evening she disturbed the neighbors so much with her rustling around that they could hardly get to sleep. Finally it got to the point where they couldn't take any more. They lay in wait for the mouse, and poured a pot of hot water after it as it vanished into a hole. The next morning the girl's mother wailed because her daughter had scalded herself. So the neighbors knew for sure who the little mouse had been and from that point on had their peace and quiet.

Die Mitternachtsmesse

Einst kam ein junger Geistlicher nach Lohr, wo ihm von einer saltsamen Erscheinung berichtet wurde. Um Mitternacht, so erzählten ihm die Leute, erscheine ein Priester in der Stadtpfarrkirche und lese die heilige Messe. „Das will ich mir einmal anschauen", sagte der junge Geistliche, und meinte weiter, er werde der seltsamen Erscheinung ministrieren. Kurz vor Mitternacht ging er in die Stadtpfarrkirche. Als nun die Glocke zwölf geschlagen hatte, soll sich die Sakristeitür wie von Geisterhänden geöffnet haben und ein Priester feierlich und ganz langsam zum Altar geschritten sein, wo er dann anschließend die heilige Messe gelesen habe. Der neue Stadtpfarrer hat ministriert. Nach der heiligen Messe soll sich der geheimnisvolle Priester vor ihm noch verneigt haben. Nach einem gemurmelten „Vergelt's Gott für den Ministrantendienst!" sei er wieder verschwunden. Die Sage weiß weiter zu melden, daß der geheimnisvolle Geistliche nie mehr erschienen sei. Die Haare des neuen Stadtpfarrers aber sollen am nächsten Morgen grau gewesen sein. Von da an nannten ihn die Leute Pfarrer „Grau", wie er auch in alten Urkunden verzeichnet steht.

27 The Midnight Mass

Once a young clergyman came to Lohr, where a strange apparition was reported to him. At midnight, so the people told him, a priest would appear in the town parish church and say holy Mass. "That I'd like to see!" replied the young clergyman, adding that he intended to serve this apparition as an altar boy. Shortly before midnight he went into the parish church. Now, when the bell had struck twelve, the sacristy door supposedly opened, as though by ghostly hands, and a priest solemnly and slowly walked to the altar and then said Mass. The new pastor served as altar boy. After the Mass was over, the mysterious priest supposedly bowed to him. After murmuring, "Thanks for serving my Mass," he disappeared, they say. People who tell this tale claim to have knowledge that the mysterious clergyman never appeared again. The next morning, however, the hair of the new pastor was reportedly gray. Thereafter the people called him "Father Gray," as it is recorded also in the old documents.

Die schwarze Katze im Pferdestall

In der Gertraudgasse zu Würzburg war ein Stall, dort ging es nicht mit rechten Dingen zu. An manchem Morgen waren den Pferden die Schwänze zu festen Zöpfen geflochten, die Tiere schwitzten und zeigten sich ängstlich und unruhig. Und immer wenn das geschah, trieb sich eine schwarze Katze im Stall herum. Wieder einmal stampften die Pferde unruhig, und ihre Schwänze waren eng geflochten. Da fingen die Leute die Katze ein und prügelten sie ganz jämmerlich. Als tags darauf eine alte Frau, die öfters zum Betteln kam, mit vielen Verbänden daherhinkte, ahnten die Leute, wer die schwarze Katze gewesen sei. Im Pferdestall aber war seit der Zeit Ruhe.

28 The Black Cat in the Horse Stable

On Gertrude Street in Würzburg there was a stable where strange things happened. Many a morning the tails of the horses were twisted into tight plaits, and the animals sweated and acted nervous and restless. Whenever that happened, there was always a black cat prowling around in the stable. When, once more, the horses pawed at the ground nervously and their tails were braided tight, the people caught the cat and gave it a terrible beating. The next day, when an old woman who often came to beg hobbled along covered with bandages, the people had a hunch who the black cat might have been. Ever since then, it has been peaceful in the horse stable.

III Saints, Holy Days, Special Liturgical Days

Die Dräutleinsäpfel zu Lohr

Man erzählt, daß in der Nähe der Stadt Lohr vor Zeiten ein paar Apfelbäume standen, die alljährlich in der Christnacht Blüten und Früchte trugen. Die Äpfel wurden am Weihnachtsmorgen auf dem Schnee liegend gefunden; man nannte sie zu Ehren der heiligen Gertrud Dräutleinsäpfel. Um hinter die Ursache dieses Naturwunders zu kommen, stellte man einmal in einer Heiligen Nacht Wächter an die Bäume; da blieben diese ohne Blüte und Frucht. Doch das Wunder wiederholte sich, als man im Jahr darauf die Bäume unbewacht ließ. 1680 wurde über die seltsamen Bäume nach Würzburg berichtet. Aus dem dortigen Jesuitenkolleg und aus der Abtei Neustadt kamen Priester nach Lohr, um den Fall zu untersuchen. Was sie dabei herausgefunden haben, ist jedoch nicht überliefert.

29 Trudy's Apples at Lohr

It is said that once upon a time in the vicinity of Lohr stood some apple trees that blossomed and bore fruit every year on Christmas Eve. The apples were found lying in the snow on Christmas morning and were named Trudy's apples in honor of St. Gertrude. To discover the cause of this marvel of nature, watchmen were once placed near the trees on Christmas Eve, but that year they remained blossomless and fruitless. Nevertheless, the miracle occurred again the next year when the trees were left unguarded. In 1680 a report about the unusual trees was sent to the Bishop of Würzburg. Priests from the Jesuit college there and from Neustadt Abbey came to Lohr to investigate the situation. Whatever they discovered in their investigation, however, has remained a secret.

Das Sackenbacher Ringlein

Oberhalb Sackenbach suchte vor Jahren eine Frau aus dem Ort Heidelbeeren. Mitten im Pflücken hörte sie auf einmal ein Weinen im Gebüsch und entdeckte beim Nachschauen einen zarten blonden Knaben, der einen blitzenden Ring an der Hand trug. Die Frau nahm sich seiner an und gab ihm von der Milch zu trinken, die sie in ihrer Flasche mitführte. Das Kind trank und hörte auf zu weinen. Die Frau spielte noch ein wenig mit ihm und suchte dann weiter Beeren, immer mit dem Gedanken, das Kind mit nach Hause zu nehmen. Als sie wieder zurückkam, fand sie nur noch die leere Milchflasche und den Ring daneben, als habe ihn der liebe Gott zur Belohnung für ihre Barmherzigkeit da hingelegt. Der Ring vererbte sich von Generation zu Generation.

30 The Little Sackenbach Ring

Above Sackenbach years ago a woman from the village was looking for blueberries. While she was picking she heard crying in the bushes and, after looking around, discovered a gentle blond boy with a flashing ring on his hand. The woman picked him up and gave him some milk to drink from the bottle she'd brought along. The child drank and stopped crying. The woman played with him a little while and then looked for some more berries, thinking that she would bring him home with her. When she came back she found only the empty bottle and the little ring, as if God had laid it down there as a reward for her charity. The ring was passed down as an heirloom from generation to generation.

Aus Kohlen wurden Taler

Einst brach ein Fuhrmann in aller Morgenfrühe von Frammersbach auf, um nach Lohr zu fahren. Als er an den „Steinernen Heiligen" kam, sah er am Wege einen Haufen Kohlen. Er wunderte sich, daß sie noch so hell glühten, denn er meinte, sie stammten von einem Feuer, das die Dorfbuben tags zuvor geschürt hatten. Mit dem Fuß stieß er unter den Haufen und nahm sich eine Kohle heraus, um sich seine Pfeife damit anzuzünden. Als es Tag geworden war, hatte er einen harten Taler auf seiner Pfeife liegen. Sogleich kehrte er um, doch als er an die Stelle kam, war der Kohlenhaufen verschwunden. Im Gras daneben aber lagen so viele Taler verstreut, wie er mit seinem Fuß Kohlen aus dem Haufen gestoßen hatte.

31 From Coals Came Talers

Once a carter set out very early in the morning from Frammersbach to drive to Lohr. When he came to the landmark "The Stone Saint," he saw a pile of coals on the road. He was surprised that they were still glowing so brightly, for he supposed that they came from the fire that the village boys had kindled the day before. He kicked the pile, took up a coal, and lit his pipe. When day broke, he found he had a hard taler coin placed on his pipe. He turned around immediately but the pile of coals had disappeared. Strewn about in the grass, however, were just as many talers as pieces of coal he had kicked out of the pile.

Würzburger Wahrzeichen

Auf der Wörzborger Brucka steha zwelf große Heiligebilder. Wenn vor alters a Handwerksborsch von Wörzborg nach Karstatt kumma is, is er auf der Polezei dort g'fragt worn: „Was mache die Heilige auf der Brucka in Wörzborg?" Und wenn er nit hat sag kenn: „Sie mache a Dutzend", so ham s'en no emol nach Wörzborg zeruckg'schickt, daß er die Stadt Wörzborg kennalern kennt.

On the Würzburg bridge stand twelve large saints' images. In the old days, if a traveling apprentice came from Würzburg to Karlstadt, he was there asked by the police, "What do the saints on the bridge make?" And if he could not say "They make a dozen," he was sent back to Würzburg to familiarize himself better with the city.

Pippin auf der Brücke zu Würzburg

Auf der Mainbrücke zu Würzburg steht eine Statue des heiligen Pippin, die bei den alten Würzburgern in hohen Ehren stand. Es soll nämlich der heilige Pippin an dieser Statue guten Rat und Aufklärung erteilt haben. Hatte ein Bürger eine häusliche Angelegenheit, in der er des Rates bedurfte, so ging er abends auf die Brücke und betete dreimal: „O heiliger Pippinus, was soll ich tun?" Und bis zum anderen Morgen hatte ihm der heilige Pippin guten Rat gegeben, und er wußte, welchen Entschluß er fassen solle. Daher hört man noch heute die Würzburger sagen, wenn einer nicht recht schlüssig werden kann: „Geh auf die Brücke und befrage den heiligen Pippinus!"

33 Pippin on the Bridge at Würzburg

On the Main bridge at Würzburg stands a statue of Saint Pippin, who was held in high regard by the old inhabitants. For at this statue Pippin is supposed to have given good advice. If a citizen had a domestic concern for which he was in need of advice, he went to the bridge in the evening and prayed three times, "Oh Saint Pippin, what should I do?" And by the next morning St. Pippin would give him good advice, and he would know which decision to make. As a result, today one can still hear the people of Würzburg say, if someone is uncertain about something: "Go to the bridge and ask St. Pippin!"

Die Burkardswecken

Der heilige Burkard, der der erste Bischof von Würzburg gewesen ist, ließ einst während einer Hungersnot bei einem Bäcker Wecken backen und sie täglich unter die armen Leute verteilen. Deshalb feierte das Würzburger Volk lange Zeit hindurch seinen Jahrestag am 14. Oktober mit einer alten Sitte: Es wurden von den Bäckern Wecken von einer eigenen Form, nämlich der eines Ringes, am Festtag des heiligen Burkard unter dem Namen Burkardswecken gebacken, und Freunde, die sich zufälligerweise an diesem Tag begegneten, grüßten sich um einen Burkardswecken, den derjenige bekam, der dem anderen mit dem Gruße: „Guten Morgen um einen Burkardswecken" zuvorgekommen war.

Jetzt werden solche Burkardswecken von den Bäckern im sogenannten Burkarder- oder Mainviertel noch gebacken; aber die Sitte, diese zu verschenken, ist außer Brauch gekommen.

34 The Burkhard's Rolls

Once, during a famine, Saint Burkhard, who was the first Bishop of Würzburg, had rolls baked by a baker and given to the poor every day. For a long time, therefore, the people of Würzburg celebrated his feastday, the fourteenth of October, with an old custom. Rolls of a distinctive shape, a circle, were baked by bakers on the feast day of St. Burkhard and called "Burkhard's Rolls." Friends who accidentally met on this day greeted one another for a Burkhard's Roll—won by the person who was the first to give the greeting, "Good morning for a Burkhard's Roll."

These Burkhard's Rolls are still available in bakeries in the so-called Burkhard- or Main-Quarter of the city; but giving them away is no longer a custom.

Das Juliusspital unter höherer Obhut

Jedes Jahr in einer heiligen Nacht kommt der selige Bischof Julius in das Spital, welches er zu Würzburg gestiftet hat und erteilt ihm seinen Segen. Bei seiner Ankunft tun sich die Torflügel von selbst auf. Als einst die Spitalvorsteher eine üble Wirtschaft führten, fanden sie zwei Morgen nacheinander in ihrem Zimmer eine frisch geschriebene Weisung des längst verstorbenen Stifters, wie die Verwaltung geschehen solle. Da sie einen Betrug vermuteten, ließen sie in der nächsten Nacht die zwölf ältesten Männer des Spitals in dem Zimmer wachen. Auf einmal trat der selige Bischof Julius herein, schrieb etwas nieder und entfernte sich dann. Am Morgen meldeten die Männer den Vorstehern die Erscheinung und übergaben ihnen das Geschriebene, welches nochmals die vorige Weisung enthielt. Nun suchten die Vorsteher ihren Fehler wieder gutzumachen und ihr Amt nach Pflicht und Gewissen zu verwalten. Wenn die Leute im Spital weniger als das vorgeschriebene Essen erhalten, so lärmt es nachts in der Küche, als wenn alle Kessel durcheinandergeworfen würden.

35 The Julius Hospital under Higher Protection

Every year on a holy night the blessed Bishop Julius comes into the hospital which he founded in Würzburg and gives it his blessing. Upon his arrival the wings of the gate open by themselves. Once when the hospital directors were mismanaging the place, they found in their room two mornings in a row a freshly written directive from the long-dead founder about how the management should be handled. Since they presumed it was a hoax, the next night they had the twelve oldest men of the hospital stand guard in the room. All of a sudden blessed Bishop Julius stepped in, wrote something down, and departed. In the morning the men reported the apparition to the directors and handed over to them the writing containing the very same directive. Now the directors sought to make amends for their blunder and to discharge the responsibilities of their office and abide by their conscience. Whenever the people in the hospital receive less than the prescribed amount of food, at night it sounds like all the cauldrons and kettles are being thrown about the kitchen.

Macarius trank keinen Wein

Macarius, ein Mönch aus dem Schottenkloster in Regensburg, wurde Abt des Schottenklosters St. Jakob in Würzburg. Eines Tages rief der Bischof Embrico den Abt zu sich. Als Wein aufgetragen wurde, entschuldigte sich der fromme Mann, er trinke keinen Wein. Der Bischof schüttelte den Kopf, und sagte dann lächelnd: „Ich befehle dir aus heiligem Gehorsam, bitte dich auch, daß du zu Ehren des heiligen Kilian mit mir etwas von diesem Wein kostest."

Da saß Macarius nun, zwischen Gehorsam und Gelübde schwankend. Eine Weile verharrte er still. Dann griff er zum Becher, trank einen Schluck und sagte: „Hochwürdiger Vater, ihr werdet aus gleicher Lieb euch gefallen lassen, mir aus diesem Becher Bescheid zu tun." Embrico kostete aus dem Becher des Abtes und merkte, daß darin blankes Wasser war. Er rief seinen Mundschenk, aber der beteuerte hoch und heilig, er habe vom besten Wein im Keller eingeschenkt. Da erkannte der Bischof das Wunder und neigte sich vor dem frommen Mann.

36 Macarius Drank No Wine

Macarius, a monk from the Benedictine monastery in Regensburg, became abbot of St. James's Monastery in Würzburg. One day the Bishop, Embrico, called in the abbot. When wine was served, the pious man excused himself; he did not drink wine. The Bishop shook his head and said, smiling, "I command you out of holy obedience, and I also request, that you taste some of this wine with me in honor of Saint Kilian."

At this point Macarius sat there, wavering between obedience and vow. He stayed quiet for a while. Then he grasped the mug, drank a swallow, and said: "Right reverend Father, you will surely, out of equal love, allow yourself to drink to me out of this mug." Embrico sipped from the mug of the abbot and noticed that there was clear water in it. He called his cupbearer, who swore by everything high and holy that he had filled the mug with the best wine from the cellar. The Bishop then recognized the miracle and bowed down before the pious man.

Der Fronleichnamsbock

Um das Jahr 1820 herum jagten am Fronleichnamstag Haßfurter Jäger bei Prappach und erlegten einen starken Rehbock. Nach der Jagd versammelte man sich in Prappach in der Wirtschaft. Als die Treiber den Bock brachten, eilten alle zur Tür der Gaststube hinaus. Dabei entlud sich einem Jäger das Gewehr. Der Schuß traf einen der Jagdkameraden, einen Arzt aus Haßfurt, so unglücklich in den Leib, daß er bald darauf starb.

Im folgenden Jahr, am gleichen Tag, spazierte während der Prozession ein starker Rehbock durch die Hauptstraße von Haßfurt bis zu dem Haus des Jägers, der den unglücklichen Schuß getan hatte. Der Mann holte seine Flinte, und feuerte zweimal auf den Bock vor seinem Haus. Doch der blieb unversehrt, machte dann kehrt und war plötzlich den Augen aller entschwunden.

37 The Corpus Christi Buck

On Corpus Christi around 1820 some Hassfurt hunters were out near Prappach and killed a huge roebuck. After the hunt people got together in the inn at Prappach. When the beaters arrived with the buck for all to see, the people rushed out the door of the barroom. In the pushing and shoving, the gun of one of the hunters accidentally went off. The shot so wounded one of his hunting mates, a doctor from Hassfurt, that the man soon died.

The next year during the procession, on the very same day, a huge roebuck came walking down the main street in Hassfurt to the house of the hunter who had fired the unlucky shot. The man grabbed his gun and fired twice at the buck right in front of his house. The buck, however, was left unscathed, made a quick turn, and disappeared right before the eyes of the whole community.

Der Jäger im Schönrainwald

Im „Hoffeld", dem Wald hinter Schönrain, stand einst eine große Eiche, in die ein Heiligenbild eingelassen war. Es war von einem Jäger gestiftet worden. Der Grund dafür war folgender: Eines Tages schoß der Jäger ein Wildschwein an, es hatte aber noch Kraft genug, ihn zu verfolgen. Da dem Jägersmann Pulver und Blei ausgegangen waren, rannte er zu einer Eiche. Dort fand er ein Loch im Stamm und konnte hineinklettern. Zum Dank für seine Rettung stellte er später eine Heiligenfigur in das Loch. Als die Eiche gefällt wurde, nagelten die Holzfäller die Figur an eine andere, junge Eiche. Von dort verschwand sie eines Tages und ward bis heute nicht mehr gefunden.

38 The Hunter in the Schönrain Forest

In the "Hoffeld," the forest behind Schönrain, there once stood a great oak into which a saint's image had been set. This had been given by a hunter. His motivation was as follows: One day this hunter wounded a wild boar which had enough strength left to chase him. Since the hunter had run out of powder and lead, he ran to an oak. There he found a hole in the trunk and was able to climb in. In thanks for being saved he later placed a saint's image in the hole. When the oak was felled, the woodcutters nailed the image to another, young oak. It disappeared from there one day and to this day has never been found.

Der Geisterzug aus der Ritterkapelle

In der Nacht vor dem Georgitag erhebt sich gegen Mitternacht aus der Ritterkapelle zu Haßfurt ein großer Zug von Rittern. Sie kommen in ihren blinkenden Harnischen, gerüstet mit Schild, Schwert und Speer: es sind die Geister aller fränkischen Ritter, deren Wappen wir in der Ritterkapelle in Stein gehauen erblicken. Sie ziehen mit sausendem Waffengeklirr durch die benachbarten Eichenforste in ein Tal des Steigerwaldes. Dort wird ein großes Turnier abgehalten wie in den alten, schönen Tagen der Ritterzeit. Erst beim Hahnenruf kehrt der Zug wieder zurück und trägt in seiner Mitte die verwaiste Krone des heiligen Römischen Reiches deutscher Nation.

39 The Ghostly Procession from
   the Knights' Chapel

The night before St. George's Day about midnight a large procession of knights arises out of the Knights' Chapel in Hassfurt. They come in their gleaming suits of armor, equipped with shield, sword, and lance: they are the ghosts of all the Franconian knights whose coats-of-arms we see carved in stone in the Knights' Chapel. They proceed with a blustering clash of arms through the neighboring oak forests to a valley of the Steigerwald. There they hold a great tournament as in the beautiful old days of chivalry. Not until cockcrow does the procession turn back again, carrying in its midst the orphaned crown of the Holy Roman Empire.

IV Tales Historical and Etiological

Das „Bildle" in Lohr

In Lohr, kurz vor der Einbiegung der Fahrgasse zur alten Mainfähre, steht eine Kapelle mit dem Namen „Breitenbachkapelle", auch das „Bildle" gennant. Von dieser Kapelle erzählt man folgende Geschichte:

Vor vielen Jahren haben Bewohner des Ortes an der Stelle, wo sich heute die Kapelle erhebt, wunderbaren Gesang vernommen. Dies wiederholte sich öfters, wurde von mehreren Leuten gehört, und niemand konnte dafür eine Erklärung geben, da nichts als eine verfallene Mauer dastand. Bei näherem Hinhören war man überzeugt, daß die fremden Stimmen aus der Mauer kämen. Man wollte nun der Sache auf den Grund gehen, brach die Mauer ab und stieß dabei auf ein Muttergottesbild in einer ausgesparten Nische. Gläubige Bürger von Lohr brachten das Bild in die Kirche, doch tags darauf stand es wieder auf seinem alten Platz draußen bei den Mauerresten. Dies wiederholte sich mehrmals. So kam es, daß die Leute das als Zeichen verstanden und dem „Bildle" einen würdigen Platz auf einer Säule an der Stelle gaben, wo es gefunden worden war.

Jahre nachdem sich dies zugetragen hatte, bedrohte Hochwasser das Städtchen. Besonders besorgt waren zwei Brüder namens Endres, denn sie hatten größere Mengen Holz in der Mainlände gelagert. Es sollte mit Flößen und Schiffen mainabwärts gebracht werden. In ihrer Not gelobten die beiden, für das „Bildle" eine würdige Kapelle dort zu bauen, wo es bislang am Wegrand stand. Wie durch ein Wunder richtete das Hochwasser kaum Schaden an. Daraufhin lösten die Brüder das Versprechen ein und errichteten die Kapelle. In ihr ist noch heute das Datum 1757 zu lesen, das Jahr, in dem dies geschehen ist. Die Kapelle ist seitdem Zuflucht für viele Bedrängte geworden, besonders gerne suchen Schiffer sie auf.

40 The Votive Image in Lohr

In Lohr, just before the bend in the approach road to the Main ferry, stands a chapel with the name "Breitenbach Chapel." It's also called the "Votive Image." About this chapel people tell a story as follows:

Many years ago residents of the settlement heard marvelous singing on the site where the chapel stands today. This happened repeatedly and was heard by several folks, but nobody could explain it because nothing but a ruined wall stood there. After listening more closely, people decided the strange voices came from the wall. Determined to get to the bottom of the matter, they took the wall apart and in doing so came upon an image of the Mother of God in a hollow niche. Devout citizens of Lohr took the image into the village church, but the next day it stood once again where it had been before. This happened again and again. Eventually the people took that as a sign and gave the Votive Image a worthy place on a pillar at the site where it had been found.

Years after this all happened, high water threatened the little town. Two brothers by the name of Endres were especially anxious, for they had stacked a large amount of timber near the banks of the Main that was supposed to be brought down the river by rafts and ships. So threatened, they both vowed they would build a worthy chapel for the Votive Image where, up to then, it had stood by the wayside. As if by a miracle, the high water did hardly any damage. The brothers therefore honored their pledge and erected the chapel. Today the date 1757, the year this happened, can be seen inside the chapel, which has become a refuge for many in distress. Riverfolk in particular like to seek it out.

Die Glocke zu Lohr

Einst hatte sich ein Graf von Rieneck im Spessart verirrt. Er lief kreuz und quer durch Gestrüpp und Dickicht, kam jedoch nirgends hin, wo er einen Weg aus dem Walde gefunden hätte. Und er rief so und so oft vergeblich nach Hilfe; es hörte ihn kein Mensch. Dabei war die Nacht gekommen, der Waldkauz schrie, die Baumwipfel begannen unheimlich zu rauschen, und es wurde so finster, daß man die Hand nicht vor den Augen sah. Der Graf ließ sich an einem Baumstamme nieder, um den Morgen abzuwarten. Er konnte vor Erregung kein Auge schließen die lange, lange Nacht. Endlich graute der Tag, und der Rienecker wußte immer noch nicht, wo er sich befand. Da, hörte er recht? Von weitem ertönte Glockenklang; der hallte allerdings nur schwach heran, aber der Verirrte achtete genau, von welcher Richtung er kam, ging dem Schall der Glocke entgegen und gelangte so glücklich aus dem Gewirr des Waldes heraus auf einen Weg, der nach Lohr führte. Es war eine Lohrer Glocke, die durch ihr Läuten den Grafen von Rieneck aus der Irre geleitet hatte. Der Graf bat hierauf den Kurfürsten Konrad von Mainz, eine Verordnung zu erlassen, es möge auch in der Nacht durch das Läuten mit der Glocke ein Zeichen gegeben werden, damit die Reisenden wüßten, daß sie nicht allzuweit von einem Orte wären.

Und so geschah es bis in die letzte Zeit. Die Lohrer Rathausglocke wurde jeden Abend um acht Uhr eine Viertelstunde lang geläutet. Sie ist eine der ältesten Glocken der Stadt und wurde 1453 von Kunrad Nürnberger gegossen.

41 The Bell at Lohr

Once a Count of Rieneck got lost in the Spessart. He walked back and forth in every direction, through brush and thicket, but couldn't find a path to lead him out of the forest. He cried out for help over and over; not a soul heard him. By then night had fallen, the owls were crying, the treetops began to rustle eerily, and it was growing so dark that he couldn't see his hand in front of his eyes. The Count sat himself down by a treetrunk, to await the morning. He was so upset he couldn't close his eyes the whole long night. Finally day broke, but he still didn't know where he was.

There, was he hearing right? From far away the sound of bell-ringing reached him ever so faintly; but the lost wanderer noted carefully which direction it came from, walked toward the sound, and finally found a path which led from the labyrinth of the forest to Lohr. It was the ringing of a Lohr bell which had rescued the Count of Rieneck from his wandering. Afterward the Count requested the Elector Conrad of Mainz to issue an ordinance for the ringing of bells, even at night time, as a signal for travelers so they might recognize that they weren't very far from a settlement.

And so it was done, until recently. The town hall bell at Lohr was rung each evening at eight o'clock, for a quarter of an hour. It is one of the oldest bells in the town and was cast in 1453 by Conrad Nürnberger.

Mord in Fässern

Im Jahr 1525, als der Bauernkrieg in Franken wütete, kamen Aufständische und plündernde Scharen auch nach Schönrain, das zwischen Gemünden und Lohr am linken Mainufer lag. Sie besetzten es, vertrieben die Bewohner, nahmen an sich, was nicht niet- und nagelfest war, und machten das Gebäude und seine Umgebung zu ihrem Unterschlupf. Von dort aus überfielen sie sogar zwischen Nantenbach und Neuendorf Schiffe, die reich beladen den Main hinauf oder hinab fuhren. Die Ladung raubten sie und schleppten sie mit den Gefangenen zur Schönrain. Für sie forderten sie hohes Lösegeld. Wurde es nicht bezahlt, steckte man die Unglücklichen in Fässer, die innen mit Nägeln beschlagen waren und rollte sie in einem unterirdischen Geheimgang hinab in den Main.—Noch in unseren Tagen wollen einige Bewohner dieser Gegend zu nächtlicher Stunde ein Rollen und Donnern unter der Erde gehört haben.

42 Murder in Barrels

In 1525, while the Peasants' War raged in Franconia, the revolutionaries and pillaging troops came also to Schönrain, which lay between Gemünden and Lohr on the left bank of the Main. They took it over, drove out the residents, took for themselves anything that wasn't nailed down, and made the buildings and surroundings their hideout. From this vantage they raided ships loaded with riches sailing between Nantenbach and Neuendorf. They stole the cargo, hauled it with their captives to Schönrain, and demanded a high ransom for these prisoners. If it wasn't paid, they stuffed the poor wretches into barrels studded with nails on the inside and rolled them through a secret underground passageway down into the Main. Even today some people who live in the region claim they have heard, during the night, rolling and thundering under the earth.

Der Agel-Orden

Zu Königsberg war vor alters auch ein Nonnenkloster, das hat nahe bei der Gottesackerkirche gestanden und war bereits 1269 begründet, und es hatten Mönche des Augustinerordens in Besitz. Darauf tat sich 1391 zu Königsberg eine Schwesternschaft frommer andächtiger Frauen zusammen; diese Schwesternschaft nannte sich zur Agelblume und wandte dem Kloster ansehnliche Gaben zu. Es durften nach den Ordensstatuten der Schwestern nicht über 31 sein, und die 31. hieß die Königin, welche nach ihrem Ableben durch eine neugewählte ersetzt wurde. Zum Ordenshabit gehörte notwendig eine silberne und vergoldete Akkeleiblume, welche jede gekleidete Schwester bei sich am Gewand tragen mußte, und wenn eine ohne die Blume angetroffen wurde, ward sie gebüßt um ein halbes Pfund Wachs, daraus Kerzen gefertigt wurden, welche die Strafbare vier Wochen lang vor dem Allerheiligsten während der Meßopfer anzünden mußte. Jede Schwester durfte bei ihrem Leben oder Sterben sich eine unbescholtene Nachfolgerin wählen und mußte vier Ahnen haben; daher finden sich im Ordensregister viele gräfliche und freiherrliche Frauen aus den berühmtesten fränkischen Familien, meistens Witwen.

43 The Columbine Order

Since the Middle Ages a nunnery has stood at Königsberg near the cemetery church. It was founded in 1269 and was in the possession of monks of the Augustinian order. In 1391 some pious godly women of Königsberg decided to form a sisterhood, named themselves after the columbine flower, and made sizable contributions to the cloister. According to the rules of the order, there could never be more than thirty-one nuns, and the thirty-first, called the queen, was replaced after she passed away, through an election. An essential part of the order's habit was a silver and gold columbine, which every appareled nun had to wear on her habit. If a nun was discovered without the flower, she was penalized half a pound of wax, from which candles were made and which the guilty nun had to light for four weeks before the Blessed Sacrament during the offering of the Mass. While still alive, or in her will, every nun could designate a successor of spotless reputation—who had to have four ancestors. As a result, in the order's register occur the names of many noble, aristocratic women of the most famous Franconian families, mostly widows.

Himmelszeichen

Am Montag nach Kantate [1525], es war ein heller und warmer Tag, ist doch um Mittag, als die Sonne am höchsten stand, ein schöner Regenbogen von lichten, lieblichen Farben über dem Würzburger Schloß zu sehen gewesen.

Er ist in mancherlei Weise ausgelegt worden: etlichen schien es zu bedeuten, sie möchten den aufständischen Bauern nicht entgehen und alle erschlagen werden. Andere sagten, es bedeute, daß sie beschützt und bewahrt blieben und die Bauern nicht die Oberhand gewännen.

Wie die Bauern den ersten Angriff getan, wurden sie, an 20000 Mann, von den Rittern und Herren vom Schloß abgewehrt.

Die Aufrührer hatten den Grafen Georg von Wertheim zu ihrem Anführer gewonnen, und als der an das Fallgitter trat, um das Schloß zur Übergabe aufzufordern, erblickte er den Grafen Wolf von Castell, seinen Schwager. Dieser rief ihm zu: „He, du willst unser Feind sein und ich soll bei deiner Schwester schlafen?" Doch der Wertheimer blieb auf der Seite der Bauern.

Monday following the fourth Sunday after Easter (1525) was a bright and warm day, but around noon, as the sun stood at its zenith, a beautiful rainbow of charming luminous colors could be seen above the Würzburg castle.

The phenomenon was interpreted in various ways. To many it seemed to signify that they might not escape from the rebellious peasants and would all be killed. Others interpreted it to mean that they would be guarded and protected and the peasants would not gain the upper hand.

As the peasants made the first attack, they were, some 20,000 strong, driven back from the castle by the knights and nobles.

The rebels had secured the services of Count George of Wertheim as their commander, and as he stepped up to the portcullis to demand the surrender of the castle, he caught sight of Count Wolf of Castell, his brother-in-law. The latter called out to him, "Hey, you want to be our enemy and yet I'm supposed to sleep with your sister?" But the Count of Wertheim stayed on the side of the peasants.

Der ewige Student zu Würzburg

Mancher, der nächtlicherweile an der östlichen Seite des Universitätsgebäudes vorüberging, wo oben die Gitterfenster des Karzers herabschauen, hat schon eine in einen Mantel gehüllte dunkle Gestalt die Mauer entlang auf und ab wandeln gesehen. Das ist der ewige Student.

Vor langen Jahren war einmal an der Würzburger Hochschule ein flotter Studiosus, dem Nachtschwärmereien und wüste Zechgelage zur anderen Natur geworden waren. Der Karzer war daher sehr oft seine Herberge. Da er von seinem wilden Leben durch keine Ermahnungen abzubringen war, so wurde er von seinem Vater verflucht, ewig den Studentenkarzer zu hüten. Sooft sich nun der ewige Student sehen läßt, deutet es eine neue Bevölkerung des Karzers an.

Solange aber der ewige Student nicht von seiner nächtlichen Geisterwache abläßt, so lange blüht die Alma Julia fort. Die Menschen sterben, die Wissenschaft lebt ewig.

45 The Perpetual Student at Würzburg

Many a person who's passed the eastern side of the university buildings at night, where the latticed windows of the university detention room face down, has seen a dark figure in a hooded coat ambling to and fro along the wall. This is the perpetual student.

Many years ago at the University of Würzburg there was a jolly and easy-going "student" for whom a very active night life and excessive drinking sprees had become second nature. The university detention room, where they often put him, was thus his lodging. Since even the most threatening warnings could not make him change his wild ways, his father condemned him to make the detention room his eternal home. Whenever the perpetual student is seen outside these lodgings, it means that some other good-for-nothing has displaced him.

So long as the perpetual student keeps up his nightly ghost watch, "Alma Julia," the university, continues to blossom. Human beings die, but the search for knowledge lives on!

Die Spottfiguren an der Marienkirche

Im Jahre 1397 hatte man zu Königsberg begonnen, eine neue Pfarrkirche zu errichten. Doch schritten die Bauarbeiten nur äußerst langsam voran. Der beauftragte Baumeister nämlich widmete sich seinem Werk nur eine Zeitlang, zog dann mit seinen Gehilfen weg und arbeitete anderswo. Immer wieder sandte der Rat der Stadt zum Meister Boten, die drängten und mahnten, er möchte den Kirchenbau doch endlich vollenden. Darüber entstand viel Unwillen in der Stadt, und Übles wurde dem Meister nachgeredet; vor allem zwei Ratsherren, die gegenüber der Kirche wohnten, hörten nicht auf zu schimpfen und zu schelten.

Eines Tages sah der Türmer eine große Männerschar von Haßfurt her gegen die Stadt heranrücken. Da er an einen feindlichen Überfall glaubte, blies er Alarm, und die Bürgerschaft griff zu den Waffen. Ein Bote wurde ausgesandt, nach des Haufens Begehr zu fragen. Der war höchst erstaunt, als ers statt bewaffneter Kriegsknechte eine fröhliche Arbeiterschar antraf, deren Werkzeuge in der Sonne blitzten. Es war der Kirchenbaumeister, der nicht weniger als vierhundert Gesellen heranführte. Nun ging freilich die Arbeit wacker voran. Die üblen Nachreden jedoch blieben dem Meister nicht verborgen. Er nahm auf seine Weise Rache, indem er die zwei Ratsherren, die am meisten gelästert hatten, als Spottfiguren aus dem Stein meißelte, wie sie heute noch außen an der Marienkirche zu sehen sind.

46 The Caricatures on St. Mary's Church

In 1397 construction was begun on a new parish church at Königsberg. But the construction progressed quite slowly, for the commissioned builder devoted himself to the task for only a while before leaving the site with his helpers to work elsewhere. The city council sent one messenger after another to the builder urging and reminding him that he should indeed finish the building of the church. A lot of bad feeling developed in the town, and the master was slandered. Especially the two city councilmen who lived opposite the church would not stop reviling and rebuking him.

One day the town watchman saw a large band of men advancing from Hassfurt. As he believed there was going to be a surprise attack, he blew the alarm and the citizenry took up arms. A messenger was sent out to question the intent of the gang. He was completely taken aback when, instead of armed mercenaries, he met a band of cheerful workers whose tools glinted in the sun. It was the church builder leading no fewer than four hundred journeyman workers. Now the work certainly moved along swiftly. But the slander against his name remained no secret to the master. He got his revenge by carving in stone, as buffoon-like figures, the two city councilmen who had badmouthed him the most. And these laughingstocks can still be seen today outside St. Mary's Church.

Der Lindenzweig im Seckendorfer Wappen

Durch Seckendorf kam eines Tages eine Reiterschar, unter der sich auch der Kaiser befand. Die Burschen und Mädchen tanzten gerade unter der Dorflinde. Vor den unbekannten vornehmen Herren aber wollten sie nicht weitertanzen. Ein übereifriger Herr vom Hof zischte drauf einem der Burschen zu: „Tanzt, der Kaiser steht vor euch und will es!" Im selben Augenblick scheute sein Pferd. Der Bauernbursche riß einen Zweig von der Linde und verscheuchte rasch den Mückenschwarm, der um die Nüstern des Pferdes schwirrte.

Dem Kaiser gefiel der umsichtige und beherzte junge Mann. Er nahm ihn mit, und als sich der junge Seckendorfer mit Rat und Tat bewährte, schlug der Kaiser ihn zum Ritter und gab ihm den Lindenzweig ins Wappen.

47 The Linden Twig in the Seckendorf
Coat-of-Arms

One day a cavalry troop which included the Emperor came through Seckendorf. At that moment boys and girls were dancing under the village linden tree. But they didn't want to keep on dancing in front of the distinguished men they didn't know. One overly zealous courtier hissed at one of the boys, "Dance, the Emperor is standing right in front of you and wants you to!" That very moment his horse panicked. A peasant lad tore a twig off the linden tree and quickly chased away the swarm of flies buzzing around the horse's nostrils.

The Emperor liked the prudent and spunky young man. He took him along, and when the young man from Seckendorf proved himself by word and deed, the Emperor knighted him and made the linden twig part of his coat-of-arms.

V Treasure Hunts

Der Schatz unter der Kertelbachwiese

Einst soll an der Kertelbachwiese in Lohr ein Schloß gestanden haben. Im Keller des Schlosses steht heute noch ein Kessel, der bis zum Rand mit Gold gefüllt ist. Davor sitzt ein Männlein, zählt Geld und rechnet. Dies geht schon Jahrhunderte so; das Männlein wird aber nicht älter und das Weinglas nicht leer. Zu mitternächtlicher Stunde schlägt das Männlein elf mächtige Schläge auf den Deckel des Kessels. Dabei wachen drei dunkle Gestalten in den hinteren Gewölben auf und fangen an, Felder zu messen und Grenzsteine zu versetzen. Nach getaner Arbeit berichten sie dem Männlein, das dann von neuem die ewige Rechnerei fortsetzt.—Vor Jahren wollten einmal drei wackere Burschen den Schatz heben. Ein Wirt spendierte einen guten Trunk und ein kräftigendes Essen. Da sagte einer: „Heut' packe mer'sch!" Er dachte aber an das splendide Essen. Als sich die drei an die Suche machten, fanden sie tatsächlich den Kessel, gefüllt mit Gold. Sie sahen auch die ungerechten Feldgeschworenen, die auf einem Felde ihr sonderbares Treiben unter tollen Sprüngen verrichteten. Da mußten die drei angeheiterten Schatzgräber hellauf lachen, worauf der Kessel und die bösen Gesellen verschwanden und nimmer gesehen wurden.

48 The Treasure under the Kertelbach Meadow

Once, as people believe, a castle stood on the Kertelbach meadow in Lohr. In the cellar of this castle today a kettle still stands, filled to the brim with gold. In front of it sits a dwarf counting money and figuring. Although this has been going on for hundreds of years, the little man doesn't grow older and his wineglass never empties. At midnight the dwarf strikes eleven powerful blows on the lid of the kettle. At that point three dark figures awaken farther back and begin to survey fields and change boundary stones. After they finish their work they report to the dwarf, who then recommences his endless figuring.

Many years ago three brave youths wanted to remove the treasure. An innkeeper treated them to a good drink and a nourishing meal. One of them said, "We'll get it today!"— but as he said so he was thinking about the splendid meal. As the three were later making their search, they actually found the kettle filled with gold. They also saw the unjust boundary deputies who were carrying on their odd activity while bouncing around crazily. The three tipsy treasure-diggers had to laugh out loud, whereupon the kettle and the wicked fellows disappeared and were never seen again.

Die Schatzsucher aus Halsbach

Drei Burschen aus Halsbach wollten in der Ruine Schönrain den Schatz heben. Das konnten sie aber nur an einem ganz bestimmten Tag, und sie mußten dazu frei von Sünden sein. Sie riefen deshalb die heilige Cäcilia an. Diese erschien ihnen, weinte aber bitterlich. Die Schatzgräber gingen daraufhin in die Ruine und begannen zu graben. Als sie tatsächlich auf den Schatz stießen, sahen sie, daß der Teufel mit einem Prügel auf dem Kasten saß. Er fragte: „Seid ihr von Sünde frei?"—„Ja!" Da versetzte er dem einen von den Burschen einen Schlag, daß er bis an sein Lebensende die Beule behielt. Der Mann hatte nämlich jüngst einen Sack Kartoffeln gestohlen. Daraufhin versank der Schatz wieder und ist bis heute nicht gehoben worden.

49 The Treasure-Hunters from Halsbach

Three youths from Halsbach wanted to remove the treasure in the Schönrain ruin. They could do so, however, on only a very specific day and, furthermore, had to be free from sin. They therefore appealed to St. Cecilia, who appeared to them but wept bitterly. Right away the treasure-diggers went into the ruin and began to dig. When they actually struck the treasure, they saw the devil sitting on the chest with a club in his hand. "Are you free from sin?" he asked. "Oh yes!" they replied. He then gave one of the fellows such a blow that he never did get rid of the bump. You see, he had recently stolen a sack of potatoes! Then the treasure sank back into the earth and has never been removed.

Der heiße Schatz von Schönrain

Am Fuße des Schönrainberges hüteten zwei Halsbacher Buben ihr Vieh. Dabei machten sie ein Feuer an. Am Abend aber löschten sie es nicht, und die Kohlen glühten in der Nacht weiter. Ein Schneider, der von Hofstetten nach Halsbach ging, sah die Kohlen und meinte, es wäre der Schatz von Schönrain. Schnell packte er sie in seinen Rucksack und dachte, am nächsten Tag würden sie zu Gold geworden sein. Der Schneider eilte nun nach Hause und wollte seinen Fund herzeigen. Unterwegs wurde ihm aber ganz heiß auf seinem Rücken. Er bemerkte nun, daß sein Rucksack brannte, nahm ihn ab und warf ihn in den Ziegelbach, wo er sogleich erlosch. Seit dieser Nacht gelüstete den Schneider nie mehr nach einem Schatz.

50 The Hot Treasure of Schönrain

At the foot of the Schönrain mountain two boys from Halsbach were tending their cattle. While they were taking care of the cattle they lit a fire. They did not put it out in the evening, however, and the coals continued to glow into the night. A tailor who was going from Hofstetten to Halsbach saw the coals and thought they might be the treasure of Schönrain. He quickly packed them in his knapsack and thought that the next day they would have turned into gold. He hurried home and wanted to show off his find. On the way his back started to feel very hot. He noticed that his knapsack was burning, took it off, and threw it into the Ziegel Brook, where it went out. Ever since that night the tailor has had no craving whatsoever for treasure.

Der Schatz von Raueneck

Unter den Trümmern des Bergschlosses Raueneck im Haßgau liegt ein Schatz vergraben, der von einem ruhelosen Geist bewacht wird. Auf der Mauer grünt ein Kirschbäumchen. Wenn es zu einem Baum erstarkt ist, wird es abgehauen und eine Wiege daraus gezimmert. Wer in dieser Wiege als Sonntagskind ruht, wird, wenn er reinen Herzens geblieben ist, in einer Mittagsstunde den Geist befreien und den Schatz heben. Dann ist er so reich, daß er Raueneck und alle anderen verfallenen Schlösser ringsum wieder aufbauen kann. Wenn aber das Bäumchen verdorrt oder vom Sturm gebrochen wird, muß der Geist wieder warten, bis ein Kirschkern, von den Vögeln auf die Mauer getragen, aufkeimt und aufgrünt.

51 The Treasure of Raueneck

Under the ruins of the Raueneck mountain castle in the Hassgau lies a buried treasure guarded over by a restless ghost. A cherry sapling sprouts on the wall. After it has grown into a tree, it is cut down and a cradle is built from its wood. Whoever sleeps in this cradle as a Sunday's child will, if he remains pure in heart, during the noon hour free the ghost and release the treasure. He will then be so rich that he can once again rebuild Raueneck and all the castles around. But if the sapling withers or is broken by a storm, the ghost must wait again until a cherrystone, carried by the birds upon the wall, germinates and sprouts.

Das Bestevergessen

Ein Mädchen aus Gerolzhofen arbeitete über Mittag auf dem Feld. Auf einmal stand vor ihr eine gespenstische Nonne mit einem altertümlichen Schlüsselbund in der Hand. Mit einer Handbewegung bat sie das Mädchen, ihr zu folgen. Die beiden kamen in einen Weinberg. Dort schloß die Nonne eine Tür auf und führte das Mädchen in ein unterirdisches Gewölbe voller Gold, Silber und kostbarer Geräte. Sie legte den Schlüssel neben die Schätze und sprach: „Was dir gefällt, kannst du mitnehmen. Doch vergiß nicht das Beste." Wie geblendet von dem Gefunkel und Gegleiß ringsum packte das Mädchen in seine Schürze, was ihm gerade am meisten in die Augen stach. Und als die Nonne nocheinmal mahnte, das Beste nicht zu vergessen, griff sie nach einem hübschen Geschmeide. Kaum war das Mädchen mit seinen Kostbarkeiten ins Tageslicht getreten, verschwanden Tür und Nonne, aber auch alle Schätze, die es mitgenommen hatte. Das Beste, nämlich den Schlüssel, hatte es in seiner Verblendung liegenlassen.

52 The Best Forgotten

A girl from Gerolzhofen was working in the field over the noon hour. All of a sudden a ghostly nun stood in front of her with an ancient ring of keys in her hand. With a gesture she beckoned the girl to follow her. They both came to a vineyard. There the nun unlocked a door and led the girl into an underground vault full of gold, silver, and precious things. She laid the keys near the treasures and spoke, "Whatever you like you can take with you. But don't forget the best!" As though blinded by all the glitter and glare, the girl stashed in her apron whatever attracted her most. When the nun warned her once again not to forget the best, she grabbed for some pretty jewels. The girl had barely stepped into the daylight with all her treasures when the door and the nun vanished along with all the treasures she had brought with her. The bedazzled girl had left the best lying behind—the key.

Sources

I have used the following abbreviations to identify the sources for
the legends in this book:

Gräter= Gräter, Carlheinz. *Sagen und Schwänke aus Franken*.
  Konstanz: Rosgarten Verlag, 1971.
Hinze= Hinze, Christa, and Ulf Diederichs. *Fränkische Sagen*.
  Düsseldorf/Cologne: Eugen Diederichs Verlag, 1980.
Pfeiffer= Pfeiffer, Valentin. *Spessart-Sagen*. Aschaffenburg: Paul
  Pattloch Verlag, 1972/1948.
Schickelberger= Schickelberger, Franz. *Aus alten Zeiten: Main–
  Spessart-Sagen*. Würzburg: Echter Verlag, 1977.
Treutwein= Treutwein, Karl. *Sagen aus Mainfranken*. Würzburg:
  Stürtz Verlag, 1969.
FTG after one of these source identifications indicates that the
  legend appeared, in my translation, in *Finding the Grain:
  Pioneer Journals, Franconian Folktales, Ancestral Poems* (1977),
  but has been revised for inclusion here.

1. Pfeiffer/*FTG*.	16. Schickelberger.
2. Gräter.	17. Schickelberger.
3. Gräter.	18. Treutwein/*FTG*.
4. Treutwein.	19. Treutwein/*FTG*.
5. Gräter.	20. Schickelberger.
6. Pfeiffer/*FTG*.	21. Hinze.
7. Gräter.	22. Schickelberger.
8. Treutwein/*FTG*.	23. Schickelberger.
9. Pfeiffer/*FTG*.	24. Schickelberger.
10. Treutwein/*FTG*.	25. Schickelberger.
11. Treutwein/*FTG*.	26. Gräter.
12. Schickelberger.	27. Schickelberger.
13. Gräter.	28. Treutwein/*FTG*.
14. Gräter.	29. Treutwein/*FTG*.
15. Gräter/*FTG*.	30. Schickelberger.

31. Treutwein/*FTG*.
32. Hinze.
33. Hinze.
34. Hinze.
35. Hinze.
36. Gräter/*FTG*.
37. Gräter.
38. Schickelberger.
39. Hinze.
40. Schickelberger.
41. Pfeiffer/*FTG*.
42. Schickelberger.
43. Hinze.
44. Hinze.
45. Hinze.
46. Treutwein.
47. Gräter.
48. Schickelberger.
49. Schickelberger.
50. Schickelberger.
51. Gräter.
52. Gräter.